Endorsements

"I can't think of a better person to lead this transformational project. Ashanti is the truest daddy's girl, so who better to assemble amazing Black dads to tell the story of how they raise their daughters?"

— Quincy Bryant, Entrepreneur and Songwriter

"Dr. Ashanti has done it again! Each father she selected has shared their soul in a way that heals and inspires just as she did in her memoir, *Armed to Surrender*."

— Brother Victorious Hall, Educational Consultant and Author of *Man Up-Lifting: A New Standard for Love, Leadership & Loyalty*

"Calling all Girl Dads, dads to be, and daddy's girls! Read this book now! You are not alone in this parenting journey. Read it front to back. Don't miss a page! It screams small group study and men's ministry resource."

— Minister Randall Pike, Youth Pastor, Zion Church

Girl DAD

**VOICES, LESSONS, AND REFLECTIONS
FROM BLACK MEN ON POSITIVE PARENTING**

DR. ASHANTI BRYANT FOSTER

GIRL DAD

Copyright © 2022 Ashanti Bryant Foster

All rights reserved.

Published by Publish Your Gift®
An imprint of Purposely Created Publishing Group, LLC

No part of this book may be reproduced, distributed or transmitted in any form by any means, graphic, electronic, or mechanical, including photocopy, recording, taping, or by any information storage or retrieval system, without permission in writing from the publisher, except in the case of reprints in the context of reviews, quotes, or references.

Scriptures marked NLT are taken from the New Living Translation®. Copyright © 1996, 2004, 2007, 2013 by Tyndale House Foundation. All rights reserved.

Scriptures marked NIV are taken from the New International Version®. Copyright © 1973, 1978, 1984, 2011 by Biblica, Inc.™. All rights reserved.

Scriptures marked NKJV are taken from the New King James Version®. Copyright © 1982 by Thomas Nelson. All rights reserved.

Scriptures marked KJV are taken from the Holy Bible, King James Version. All rights reserved.

Printed in the United States of America

ISBN: 978-1-64484-592-9 (print)
ISBN: 978-1-64484-593-6 (ebook)

Special discounts are available on bulk quantity purchases by book clubs, associations and special interest groups. For details email: sales@publishyourgift.com or call (888) 949-6228.

For information logon to: www.PublishYourGift.com

DEDICATION

This book is dedicated…

To the man who has been team pink since
she announced her pregnancy.

To the man who will become a father
with a woman he doesn't love.

To the child who will only be able to complete
half of their family tree at school.

To the daughter who gets butterflies when
she hears her daddy's keys at the door.

To the woman whose brother stood in to
walk her down the wedding aisle.

To the grandfather who makes the
best pancakes and ponytails.

To the husband who prayed for a boy but got a beautiful girl.

To the coach who celebrated her progress and growth.

To the son who can't wait to become
a father when he grows up.

To Cecilia Mack, who gained her wings during this project.

This one is for you.

TABLE OF CONTENTS

Foreword by Khalid Scott 1

Acknowledgements 5

Introduction 7

CHAPTER 1
Protection by Joseph O. Bryant 11

CHAPTER 2
Praise with Affirmation by Dr. Harold A. McCray, Jr. 23

CHAPTER 3
Prayer Over Everything by Deacon Jeffrey Butler 35

CHAPTER 4
Promote Perseverance by Gregory Clark 49

CHAPTER 5
Pursue the Purpose by Julius Davis 61

CHAPTER 6
Prepare to Smile by Joseph C. Bryant 75

CHAPTER 7
Pivot into Position by Philip McNair 87

CHAPTER 8
Pressure Cooker by Reginald Mack 99

CHAPTER 9
Power in the Pause by Kelly Burgess 111

CHAPTER 10
Presence over Presents by Thomas G. Warner, Jr. 127

CHAPTER 11
Prodigal Girl Dads Prosper by Dr. Charles Lucious Perry ...139

CHAPTER 12
Pay Attention by Ashanti Bryant Foster 153

Epilogue by Dr. Dimitri Conte Kornegay 167

The Girl Dad Pledge 169

The Girl Dad Playbook: Self-Coaching Questions 171

About the Authors 181

FOREWORD

"Girl Dad." What a powerful two-word phrase this is special to someone like me who takes so much pride in being a self-declared Girl Dad. I remember when I first heard the term back in February 2020 right after the tragic death of basketball legend Kobe Bryant. So many men on social media decided to participate in this touching tribute to Kobe and his daughter, who also tragically died with him. Hundreds of dads used social media outlets to post pictures of themselves and their beloved daughters using the hashtag #girldad.

I saw the abundance of pride and love in these men, especially men of color, who wanted to let the world know "I am so proud to be my daughter's dad." It was then that I had the epiphany that I was already a Girl Dad and have been one since my daughter, Anayah, was born just a few minutes past midnight on a glorious day in August of 2002.

No other role in my entire fifty-two years of living has been as significant as being a father of a beautiful daughter. I feel like I'm the walking billboard of fatherhood—at least that's what my daughter and everyone else I know tells me. I can understand why they say that. I have been blessed to be the recipient of three Father of the Year awards over the last twenty years of my daughter's life, and I've spoken about fatherhood for radio programs, workshops, and podcasts on the topic of fatherhood. I have also been a contributing writer in three books addressing the subject of fatherhood. Yes, I am a true Girl Dad!

Now that I've introduced myself to you, let me introduce by far one of the best books you'll read about Black fatherhood and especially being a Girl Dad!

Each chapter takes you on a mental journey of how these phenomenal Black men see the importance of family and especially their relationships with their daughters. I found myself laughing, crying, venting, comparing, praying, being hopeful, and smiling with pride as I read each of these Black fathers' testimonies on the love they have with their family, especially their daughters.

I absolutely loved how our lead author and daddy's girl, Dr. Ashanti Bryant Foster, has been considerate, caring, and conscious about her coordination and compilation of our Girl Dad testimonies. Many of the dads were first-time writers, and she handled each story with grace and care. She made it clear that this is a "no-judgement" zone and a place of healing and restoration. This text is for the Black father and the father figures of daughters. I encourage you to pay close attention to the message, connect, and know that you, too, are amazing.

Get ready to be taken on this emotional ride of love, learning, and raising of girls by Girl Dads and be invigorated and delighted to know that we as Girl Dads are not the unicorns that society thinks we are, but that we are essential, participatory, and present in our family's lives.

Be well,
Khalid Scott

ACKNOWLEDGMENTS

First, I thank Helen Bryant, the mother of this daddy's girl, for putting up with my crazy ideas and praying for me without ceasing. The concept of this book wouldn't exist without you giving birth to me. Thank you, Mommy! You are the ultimate daddy's girl, so I know you understand the forever bond that daughters have with their daddies.

I also acknowledge some of my favorite Daddy's Girls—Angela, Aiesha, Joy, and Christy—whose strength inspired me to push through with this project. Your daddies went to heaven during this project, but their love is forever within you. I pray for each of your daily.

The completion of this project was seamless thanks to Publish Your Gift and the amazing team. You walked our writers through every step and remained committed to my vision throughout the project. Thank you for your diligence!

I want to thank the Dr. Ashanti Says, LLC team for providing the social media marketing events for the Girl Dad Project promotion and sales and for supporting the Girl Dad Project events. Thank you for ideating with me and allowing me to serve as your CEO. Expect great things as we move forward as a team. Thank you to FOSTERVISION Media for providing our Girl Dad's fresh headshots for the book as well.

Spizzy Smoothies & Teas, thank you for supporting The Girl Dad Project through sponsorship.

Thank you to my wonderful children, better known as the Half Dozen, who are so patient when Mommy is deep into Writing Wednesday. Thank you for doing your part in the home and supporting my projects with love. QB, JZ, Marie, Belle, SJ, and BK, this one is for you!

Finally, to Joseph Oscar Bryant. Daddy, you are my everything and everything is you. Thank you for living out loud in front of me and showing me the ups and downs of life. Thank you for telling me no sometimes and thank you for making mistakes.

INTRODUCTION

The family is the first and most influential relationship in a person's life. Within that family dynamic, the father's role as it relates to the daughter has a lasting impact. Many girls learn how to, subconsciously, relate to men based on their relationships with their fathers, and that daddy-daughter discourse, or lack thereof, becomes a rehearsal of their mother's choices. Early on, daughters seek approval and affirmation from fathers, be it her pretty dress or cute new hairstyle. Every daddy's girl wants to hear daddy call her beautiful. Throughout life, that desire only intensifies as girls become women who become wives and mothers who long for that affirmation, now receiving it in various avenues.

This book is written to support fathers of all ages and stages of life while serving as a collection of stories that honor and appreciate the role of the daughter. The vision of this work is to acknowledge, appreciate, and affirm Black men who parent, coach, and support children. Fatherhood looks like providing the essentials in life, serving as a model of responsibility, and unconditional love and protecting their family.

I invite you to experience fatherhood through the personal stories of amazing men who bring vulnerability and strength to this work. It is in the storytelling that the author can also receive healing and restoration. You will read twelve stories of the various aspects of fatherhood to include single fatherhood, fathering from a distance, absent fatherhood, becoming a father at a young age, and pouring into children with prayer and praise. Perhaps you, too, have experienced some of these circumstances either as a parent, child, or supporter. As you read the message from their hearts, it is up to you to find the lesson that resonates with you the most.

If I had to guess, I'd say you selected this book because you are interested in acquiring more tips and resources to polish your fatherhood practices, getting a sneak peek into fatherhood, or even supporting an author you know. You may even be a daddy's girl or someone who longed for the father figure in your life. This book is also for you.

Each chapter provides a story of raising Black daughters, followed by a charge to the father and a letter or prayer to the daughter. If you are a daughter reading this text, I invite you to read these letters and prayers as they are written just for you. Daughters, as you read, consider how your father may have felt in difficult situations and find space in your heart to be open to new beginnings. We can't change the past, but we can surely accept the present as just that—a gift.

It is my hope that as you reflect, make connections, smile, and even shed a tear that you also come away understanding five important points in positive parenting:

- Providing presence over presents cultivate peace and protection
- Powerful prose produces those who persevere
- Prodigal fathers can still produce promise
- Persistently prioritizing their purpose welcomes the pursuit of happiness
- Practicing the posture of prayer and praise pursues God's presence

My prayer is that as this text encourages you to celebrate the voices of fatherhood, you are inspired to amplify the fatherhood in your community. Daughters, I pray that you can read and accept the words in the prayers and letters written directly to you.

As you engage in each story, note the resources in the Appendix that will guide you as you accept the charge to polish your role as Girl Dad or daddy's girl.

Chapter 1
PROTECTION

by Joseph O. Bryant

Fatherhood was something that I patiently anticipated for seven years into marriage with my high school sweetheart. Although it was highly anticipated, I had no idea how to be a father of a daughter. As a little boy in our small town in North Carolina, I was the youngest of three sons. Both of my parents had to work outside of the home, which meant my brothers and I had to do all of the chores. In our home, there was no such thing as girl chores because there were no girls! I had to do chores like cooking dinner, cleaning up the house, and gathering wood and kindling for the stove and kitchen. The three of us switched off those chores for the entire week. Between that responsibility and home economics, I learned how to cook, sew, and bake. When it was time to play, the neighbors' big field behind the house called for basketball, football, roaming in woods and campfires. One evening, when it was dark, we started a campfire. Someone, whose name I will never mention, dropped an already lit candle as we all took running in opposite directions trying to escape the rattlesnake we heard. Well, that fire lasted three or four days. 'Til this day, we will never tell who did it. But girls weren't invited to any of these adventures! In hindsight, if we had let the girls in, perhaps we wouldn't need to keep the secret about who started the fire over sixty years later.

Although we kept the girls out of our play time, everyone knew that we didn't play around when it came to outsiders trying to get to know the neighborhood girls better. They had to come through us, as we were the protectors of Mavis Road. And that protection was extended to every woman on the block to include mothers, aunts, and cousins of all ages. That is what I knew about relationships with girls: *I must protect the women around me.* My family didn't have daughters, and the fathers of daughters in the neighborhood were few. We had a lot of single mothers, fathers who had left the home, and even widows, including the mother of one of my best friends whose dad was tragically killed in a hunting accident in the woods, leaving the mom with lots of children. Needless to say, when I finally got the opportunity to be a father, I had no blueprint; I just knew I needed to protect her.

When my wife and I finally conceived my firstborn, I was a young working man in my twenties and enjoying my life with my beautiful wife. Afros, bell bottoms, and good ole '70s music was our way of life. Softball leagues, Saturday night socializing, and dancing the night away consumed our time as a young couple. What we didn't have was the ultimate product of our union together: a child; and believe me, it wasn't because of lack of trying. After a handful of years of marriage, my wife and I moved into our first single-family home in Maryland. At the time, Prince George's County was predominately white, and for a Black couple to have a home in this neighborhood was a big deal. My wife and I had spent a few years living with family members and even renting apartments in DC after coming up from North Carolina until finances and opportunity aligned to allow us to purchase our first home. This purchase was significant because it was at that time that we had a nice-sized backyard, a master bedroom, and a beautiful roomy home for the growing family we hoped to have. The day we found out we'd finally be parents was sweet music to our ears. I was overwhelmed with gratitude even though I had no idea what to expect or how to prepare. I think God was waiting for us to move into our home in Maryland before starting our family. That yellow and green edifice became the backdrop to thousands of photos taken of our first baby girl, Ashanti. In 1978, there was no gender reveal party, and it was when she was born that I knew I would become a forever Girl Dad. From that day forward, my life changed forever.

There was no way that I could wake up the next morning that summer and be the same ole Joe. The pre-fatherhood Joe would leave work and hang out an hour or two after work with his buddies, but the Girl Dad Joe couldn't wait to get home so he could spend time with his baby girl. I knew what my responsibility was, and everything I ever wanted was already at home waiting for me. My buddies, the parties, and the social life was nothing compared to my baby girl. She not only won my heart, but she also won several beautiful baby contests—the first one at the church and the second one at her Child Development Center for Queen of Kindergarten.

As a little baby, Ashanti had to be with me all the time. She loved when my attention was focused on her. I remember having to leave the house quietly, making sure that my keys and my belt buckle didn't make a noise because when it did, I knew what had to happen at that point. I needed to wait for my sidekick, Ashanti, to put her shoes on and get ready. When she was a little girl, Ashanti enjoyed riding in the White Mustang, which I purchased from my neighbor Mister Charlie, when we were out and about. She always wanted to walk on her own instead of having me hold her in my arms, which made holding hands interesting as I stand over six feet tall. Now it makes sense that she would want to go everywhere with me because for the first few years of her life, I was her childcare provider. For months at a time, in order to save on finances, my wife and I decided that Ashanti would stay with me during the day since I worked at night, and then when I went into work at 3 pm, I would take her to the babysitter for a few hours until my wife got off work and picked her up.

Now of course, I had to get some sleep as well, so my plan was to always put her in her crib for nap time and lock the bedroom door so she couldn't get out. One day, I woke up and she wasn't in the crib! I checked the door, and it was still locked. I panicked because my job was to protect her. After looking under the bed and under the crib, who did I find wedged snuggly in between the bed and the wall fast asleep? Ashanti. And that wasn't the last time that she escaped from her crib either. One day she climbed out of the crib while I was napping, went over to the dresser, and got into her mother's nail polish. Let's just say she helped me get fancy for work by giving me ten red polished fingernails while I was still asleep. I usually only had about one hour between getting ready for work and getting her ready for the babysitter, so I had no choice but to go in with red polished fingers. Needless to say, my hands spent most of the time in my pocket between sorting other people's mail by zip code.

We did more than sleep and do nails during the day. She enjoyed children's shows and the stories, or what some would call daytime soap operas. I had a 1970 Chevelle Super Sport with a huge engine, dual exhaust, and blue and white stripes that I called Hot Rod that she would hear coming into the driveway at night. When I did finally get home from work in the middle of the night, she would be the first to wake up and greet me. I'd find her standing up in the crib, refusing to go back to sleep when she heard my voice. Instead of going back to bed, she just wanted to lie on my chest. I think she was listening to my heartbeat, and it soothed her back to sleep.

On another occasion when she was about three years old, I remember Ashanti making motions with her mouth like she was speaking, but no words were coming out. She was not making a sound. All I knew was that something was wrong with my baby girl and that I needed to get her help as soon as possible. I got into the white Mustang that she loved so much and drove down to the regional hospital to see what was wrong with her. Apparently, I did not take her to the hospital that her mom preferred, but that didn't matter to me at the time. I had to protect my baby girl and get her talking again. Once we noticed her inability to express her emotions verbally, we got her the support she needed, and I made sure I paid close attention to her emotions and made sure she felt safe at all times.

Young Ashanti insisted that I do her hair and make her lunch. She required my presence in all aspects of her life, especially anything she didn't want her mom to do. As she was growing up, I could see that she had inherited the Bryant family gap in her teeth. Instead of getting upset when classmates made fun of her, she would smile hard as a badge of honor, noting that she looked just like her daddy.

As she matured into a young woman, what was consistent was her need to spend time with me and see me in the crowd whenever she was on stage. She found love in my presence and in my praise. She had to hear that she was beautiful and that she was doing a great job in whatever it was she was doing, so I made sure I loved her in the way she needed me to.

I continued to work at night even though she and her baby brother were well into secondary school. It just worked for our family dynamic and saved us lots of money in aftercare. At our house, someone was always home. I became the school chauffeur and homework helper even though there was a neighborhood bus and tutoring at school. And it was my honor to drive her around wherever she wanted to go.

I was forty-four years old with a sixteen-year-old daughter and eleven-year-old son when I received my Girl Dad promotion. I was shocked that my wife and I would conceive again after having to wait so long for our first child. Ashanti was starting to prepare for college (she would be the first in the family to attend), and my son, Joe, was making me proud by playing baseball and the drums like his daddy. I thought I was only a few years away from retirement. Life changed once again when we found out through testing that another daughter would join our family. This unexpected blessing automatically put us in the high-risk pregnancy group. I think my wife had double the amount of testing that she had had for our first two children, but the one test she refused was the amniocentesis—the test that would give us an indication of whether or not our child had Down syndrome. My wife believed that whatever God allowed is what we could handle, and she was not getting the test. She protected our daughter and her womb from having a long needle placed into her abdomen to get fluid out to test our baby. We were prepared to welcome whatever masterpiece God was developing for us. Months after conception, in late April of 1994, came my princess, and she was perfect. She quickly became a mommy's girl and spent the majority of her time shadowing her mom in ministry work and home life. One thing my little princess loved more than anyone else in the family was my cooking. She was the only one to enjoy my cooked pig feet, a Black family delicacy. I taught her how to cook scrambled eggs at a young age and of course how to ride her bike and drive a car. She always had the desire to learn essential skills so that she could activate her independence, and I was there to teach her the way. When our princess needed advice, insight, and straight talk, she came straight to me, and not much has changed twenty years later. She found love through being an apprentice and learning life from me.

Because of the large age gap between her and her siblings, she was raised like the only child of the house and had our full attention while the other two children were in Baltimore earning degrees. In her middle school years, she wanted to participate in a young women's leadership group at her school that ended with a dinner dance where the girls wore white dresses and did a dance with their fathers. I don't know what it was with that choreography because I had always been an amazing dancer and so had princess, but we could not get the steps. When it was time for the event, I told her to follow me, and we did our own dance. It was special because as long as we were on beat, we didn't worry about what everyone else was doing. As long as the goal is accomplished, sometimes marching to the beat of your own drum is more important than falling in line and being a carbon copy of everyone else.

Independence was and still is important to my princess. She has always reached higher than high to achieve the best. She earned the highest honors in Girl Scouting and college and has always exceeded expectations. As a woman, she seeks my guidance and advice about everything from taxes to buying a home to even why men do and say what they do. As her protector, I give her the truth about men. Girl Dad code is way more important than guy code any day. Ashanti didn't even get her driver's license until she was twenty-two and became a mother of her own child because she knew she could count on me to be there. Baby girl wanted my quality time and emotional attention, while my princess desired my quality time to empower and support her independence.

Baby girl and princess desired different types of love, but some training was the same. I taught them that guys calling them late at night is disrespectful, and that they shouldn't need to touch doors in the presence of males. My daughters are taught how to check their own oil in the vehicle and that love is an action, so pay attention to what people do above what they say. I modeled responsibility by going to work every day and keeping a job to support my household while doing whatever it took to make sure they had what they needed. They also learned that no one will love them more than they love themselves and that their relationship with God is the most important relationship in life.

Fathering my two daughters has been and continues to be eventful. I don't always say the right things to them, and sometimes my honesty hurts their feelings. I wasn't able to attend every event, and sometimes I say no when they really need my yes, but loving them without a limit is my specialty. Besides marrying my wife, parenting is the best experience in life. Fathering a daughter, however, humbles you. It convinces you that what once was important is really trivial. It also reminds you that one day, someone will try to love your daughter as much as you love her, so you must equip your daughter with everything she will need to know to make informed decisions and live her life as a strong, loving, independent Black woman.

In thinking about lessons learned in my pursuit of being the ultimate girl dad, I assert that just because daughters share the same mother and father doesn't mean they need to be loved and adored the exact same way. What worked for my baby girl wasn't necessary for the princess, and that's okay. Knowing their love languages and heart's desires helps dads connect and secure strong bonds with their daughters, no matter what the age. I love them equally and understand that as Girl Dads, we need to be available to listen, respect, and respond. When we listen, we hear the desires of their hearts. When we respect what we hear, we don't judge them but seek to understand their point of view and decisions. When we respond, we hold their hearts in our hand and share what they need to hear to move forward, even when it hurts. The Girl Dad's role never ends, and even though my daughters are now adults in their twenties and forties, they will always be my girls and can always call on me to do the best I can at my age. The Girl Dad Joe in his seventies is just as called upon as much as the Girl Dad Joe in his twenties was. I think they really believe I can do everything.

It doesn't matter if your daughter was a long-awaited blessing or a beautiful surprise. As Girl Dads, we must protect our daughters and listen to them so that we know how to respond to them in their uniqueness. I anxiously anticipated our first daughter and unexpectedly celebrated my last daughter. The scenario around the conception of your daughter has nothing to do with them because she had no control over it, and she should all be loved with the same whole heart. Your daughters all deserve to be loved authentically and fully.

THE CHARGE

As a Girl Dad, I will honor the uniqueness of each daughter, seeking to understand what they need and how they need it. As a Girl Dad, I will honor my daughters' presence, no matter the circumstances of their conception, and I count it an honor to serve as the protector of my children. As a Girl Dad, I will support my daughter's desire to learn and become independent knowing that I may not always be there physically to meet the need. I will affirm her when she doesn't feel as beautiful as she really looks, and I will give her the quality time she needs while modeling the behaviors that she should expect from other men. As a Girl Dad, I will give my daughter permission to meet the goal by finding the pathway that makes the most sense to them.

DEAR DAUGHTER

Dear daughter,

Even though you may have been a surprise to your father, God knew all about you. In fact, you are fearfully and wonderfully made by God, and it is He who will always be your Heavenly Father. God will always protect you. You have permission to love yourself unapologetically and choose the path that makes sense for you. Don't worry about what you didn't learn or who wasn't there at every game or recital because you are loved. Find strength and courage in knowing that you were born with a purpose that is to be fulfilled no matter what your relationship is with your father figures in life. Take the time to learn something new every day and use your voice early and often. What you have to say matters, and you deserve to be heard.

Chapter 2
PRAISE WITH AFFIRMATION

by Dr. Harold A. McCray, Jr.

Knowing who you are is half the battle in succeeding in life. My name is Dr. Harold McCray, Jr. I was born and raised in West Philadelphia, Pennsylvania. If you are from Philadelphia, it is important to let people know what area of the city you grew up in. It adds validation and can spark interesting conversations beyond cheesesteaks and the Philadelphia Eagles. I am a proud graduate of two well-known historically Black universities. My undergraduate degree came from Delaware State University. I also attended Bowie State University, where I received my masters in the arts of teaching. I also received my doctoral degree from Walden University in Educational Leadership. As life changes and we all grow, I have experienced a successful career in education with over seventeen years of experience. I have worked as a teacher, mentor, assistant principal, and I am now a proud principal in Washington, DC. My overall goal is to mentor and coach new administrators as they navigate our current state in education. I am a devoted husband, a proud father of two of the most beautiful girls, inside and out, whom you will ever meet. And while I know and have a great relationship with both of my parents, I did not grow up in a two-parent household that often gave positive affirmations needed for emotional growth.

I was nervous and filled with excitement when I found out my wife and I were having a daughter. I can remember the day exactly. I returned from a summer cookout with fraternity brothers, and my wife made a huge presentation with a private reveal for the two of us. It was on that day that I knew that my life would change forever. I secretly was also scared that my parenting skills would not be the greatest. But to be honest, that is just who I am. The fear of the unknown can overwhelm me. Not only did that overwhelm me, but two years later, we had another daughter. Here I am, the father of two girls, struggling to navigate this journey while secretly battling depression. My pain point in being a father of girls, specifically Black girls, was not understanding how my words of affirmation would impact their development.

As my girls got older, became more aware of their surroundings and who they were, and started understanding words, I started to see that they needed more than attention and love. I noticed my oldest daughter struggling with taking risks and trying new things. Instead of using positive reinforcements and encouragement, I often stood there puzzled, like I did not know what to do. My mind immediately shifted to thoughts like just trying it. Just take that step. Just go! These were all things I would tell myself in my head and never dared to say out loud or even do as a child myself. What I started to notice is that my oldest daughter was somewhat like me as a kid: smart but shy and unsure of the confidence and self-pride that exist to be able to conquer all things.

I decided that it was time for me as a father to pour those words of affirmation into my daughters, especially my oldest daughter. I made it my business to ensure I speak life to my girls. I want them to know that no matter what they do, they do not need to seek validations from others, especially a man. Society would have my girls believing that they need to look a certain way, act a certain way, or try to fit in a false reality of what life is really like because of social media platforms. My dream as their father is to ensure that I dispel the typical myths that continue to impact generations of young girls. The words of affirmation from "daddy" need to be intentional and purposeful. With the challenges I have experienced as a Black man and what I have witnessed happen to Black women, words of affirmation for my daughters were non-negotiable. I started to challenge myself daily to say words like "You are gorgeous." "I love your hair today." I even express how I feel about their talents.

The more time I spend with my daughters, the more I make sure to tell them they are special, they are smart, and that they can do it no matter what. These words are important to my children because they are looking for approval, in a sense, from their father, which I noticed has built their confidence. My daughters will sing, dance, and draw and always look to me to say, "Job well done" or "Great job." These words make a difference in how they see themselves. One big example is when my oldest daughter gets her hair done. She has to always come and show me, and her first question is "Daddy, do you like my hair?" I always reply with "It's so beautiful." Then she gives me the biggest smile and hug and says, "Thank you Da-Da." My youngest will paint a picture or do a cool move and say, "Daddy, watch this." I never knew how important my words were to them. These are the moments that matter. I say this because society does not always elevate Black girls in a positive light. My overall goal is to build their confidence and to make sure their self-esteem is high so that the terrible words society may place upon my daughters will not impact them at all. They will be secure in who they are as girls who eventually will become women.

Affirming my girls taught me the essence of building their emotional well-being. I want them to grow up and reflect that it was their father who taught them to be the best versions of themselves daily no matter what this world has to offer. I want them to see that they can battle any negative thoughts, insecurities, or even criticism because of their strong emotional health. Parenting from this lens has changed my perspective on how to raise young Black girls. I knew that I did not want to repeat old school history in what I saw growing up with young girls and their parents. The lack of affirming girls, being empathetic to their situations, and even supporting their academics are major factors in their growth. My upbringing consisted of making sure I did what my elders said, being quiet, and suppressing my feelings. Through the realm of positive parenting, I am constantly looking for creative ways to affirm my kids. I do not want my words to sound redundant, but I do want them to feel heartfelt and authentic. So, if I tell my girls there is no challenge that they cannot face and overcome, I am not erasing the idea that challenges will not arise. What I am doing is explaining to them that this too shall pass. The road will never be easy, but hopefully they have the emotional and mental capacity to pull through and achieve their own goals for their own lives.

Spending time with my daughters has also taught me the importance of affirmations and their uniqueness. Sometimes I prioritize spending time together with both girls, but those solo moments where they do not have to share my attention means the world to both me and them. I remember working late one night in Washington, DC, which is about an hour from my home. My daughter wanted to show me one of her hairstyles so badly. Now many would ask, "Why not just FaceTime her?" Unfortunately, I had a speaking engagement and could not engage in a FaceTime call. She was disappointed that I was not there, but she made sure to have my wife record and take pictures so that I could see it when I eventually came home. When my oldest daughter was born, I only stayed home for two weeks and then had to return to work. At that time, the school district I worked for did not offer an extended amount of leave for fathers. The pain I felt and experienced at not being able to bond with her was hard to process. Those few hours we spent together once I got off work did not help. It took almost ten months for her to become comfortable with me. I felt like she viewed me as a stranger. I never wanted to feel that again.

My youngest daughter had an advantage that my oldest did not. I got to spend more time home with her because she was born during the pandemic in 2020. So, working from home really helped me to bond with her. The joy that was felt by having both of my daughters home and watching them grow up right before my eyes was such a blessing. Bonding with my daughters is a top priority for me. The best thing that I can ever do with them is activities in which we all participate. This could be learning their sight words or counting. This could take the form of bedtime stories or playing together. These activities create a sense of connectedness and trust that is valuable for their growth and development. The biggest lesson of bonding with my daughters is the alone time we spend together without my wife. Every mother deserves a break, and when that happens, it gives me the opportunity to build a connection with my girls. Naturally, my daughters gravitate toward my wife. Their bond is solid. During those moments when we get together, the relationship building continues. I am teaching them to be assertive and not aggressive. I expose them to a level of trust and support that should not be compared to that of other males in their life, because I am their father. I also want to make sure that their emotional well-being and emotion regulation is strong.

Trying to carry the title of the world's greatest father (something I like to call myself) comes at a cost. There is a lot of pressure, especially as a new father of two Black girls. I want to always get it right. I want to always win and never fail as a parent. I want to always make sure my words have meaning to my daughters and that they hold them dear to their heart. I often ask myself a series of questions when I am interacting with my girls. Did I acknowledge them? How have I empowered them today? Am I providing them with my undivided attention while complimenting their beauty? These questions are enough to provide a little anxiety. One thing that has been a consistent support throughout this journey is leaning into my dad circle. Many of my friends also have children (specifically daughters), and we communicate daily. Communication includes an exchange of experiences, remedies, ideas, and tips. Sometimes there are a few comical moments that have to be shared to keep the momentum of fatherhood going.

It is easy to feel defeated in such a role with huge responsibilities. You must remember that you are human, and you will make mistakes. I have learned to understand the true gift of time and attention. Never take a moment, interaction, or opportunity to pour into your daughters for granted. One thing

I do immediately when I see my girls is ask about their day. What made it special? I invest some time in the conversation. Then I always affirm their responses and validate with verbal love. Sometimes that also includes our kiss-hug-and-hi-five combo. While we as adults may understand that love is understood and does not always deserve an action, I feel it is important as men that we affirm that love to our children. Our daughters need us to affirm them. Through affirmation, we can potentially disrupt their negative thoughts and help them manage and regulate their emotions. For any dad who struggles with this, remember that there are quick and easy ways to make sure our words have meaning and that we speak life into our little ladies. Start with morning affirmations. Greet your children with warm words and expressions that are so exaggerated they feel special. Even if you struggle with words, there are other ways we as fathers can affirm our daughters. The goal is to provide positive compassion. Another way to affirm your children is by validating who they are and speaking positive, encouraging words to them. Allow them to express themselves and how each thought they speak and share makes them feel. Even the most stressful situation for your daughter can be changed into a lighter one if we only take the chance to teach them how to think positive. Please understand that positive thoughts are connected to the words of affirmations we speak to our daughter. How we speak to them, especially when they are young, in my opinion, teaches them how they will see themselves. Our daughters will then become accustomed to how a man should speak to a woman, and as they grow older their standards will already be set high because of the model we provided as fathers.

THE CHARGE

As a Girl Dad, I will share positive affirmation frames with my daughters as they grow older. We will say them together as a family. I believe through providing examples and repetition, they will start to live what they say. For example, the phrase "I am enough," is a perfect way to explain to your daughters that no matter what society says you should be doing or need to look like, know that the choices you made work for you! Another affirmation I would like to share with them is "I believe in myself!" The thought of teaching this to my girls gets me excited. They are already growing into these independent young ladies, and I want them to know that it starts with the belief that they can. Once I continue to affirm them with this positive framing of believing that they have what it takes to be whoever they are, I know my daughters will be successful in life. As fathers, we are the number-one example of how a man should interact with a female. They watch everything we do and speak. We hope and pray that one day they choose to live up to these words and make us proud. Continue to pour into them and never give up. Even on the hard days, remind them that they are loved, that they mean the world to you, and that nothing will stand in the way of your love, guidance, and protection.

DEAR DAUGHTER

Daughters, never forget who you are in all that you do. Remain true to yourself and know that integrity will get you a lot further in life than trying to be a carbon copy of someone else. I have learned so much about myself as a man because of you. I pray that the lessons you continue to teach me make me a better father. I hope that the love you give and the patience and support I provide, mixed with some compassion, lets you know that I care about you deeply. The time we spend together motivates me to work hard so that you can have the life that you deserve. I want you to be comfortable coming to me at all times. I want you to know that as long as I have breath in my body, I will do all I can to protect you, guide you, and love you. Good, bad, or indifferent, my love will always remain unconditional. Be the beautiful souls that God has sent you here to be. Advocate for your emotional and mental health. Dream big and achieve often. The sky really is the limit. Stay firm in the foundation we provide you both and go forth and serve in this society. Know that I will do all I can to not allow any danger to come your way.

DEAR AVA AND ARYANA

From the day both of you were born, I knew that my life would change forever. You have changed me more than you will ever know. You both taught me what love looks like without conditions. I am so blessed to be your father. Each day that I face this world, you are always in the front of my mind. I pray that I make you proud. I hope that you find peace and security within me. You both are so intelligent and beautiful. Never forget it. Each of you has a uniqueness about you that you must always embrace.

You mean more to me than life itself. If you ever need me, I will always be there for you.

Love,
Your Daddy

Chapter 3
PRAYER OVER EVERYTHING

by Deacon Jeffrey Butler

As a young man growing up in a middle-class family, I was the son of an Army veteran who grew up in South Carolina. My dad, Junis Butler, did not have daughters but two sons, so I did not have examples of or exposure to how a father should raise Godly daughters. After a life of raising both of my daughters, it is only by God's grace and mercy that they have become the young women that they are. It is through this writing that God has allowed me to open my emotions and heart to them. This venue allows me to tell them how much I truly love them. The biggest impact on my life was finding a church home. It was in the church that I found my bride, had my children baptized, and served in the Ministry.

I said yes to this project so that there will never be any doubt of how much my daughters mean to me. I prayed for an opportunity to raise children since I was sixteen years old. As a teenager, I would admire dads who were playing with their children on the playground, and I always wanted to feel that same joy. God answered my prayers and blessed me with three beautiful children: Christina, Crystal, and Jeffrey. God has truly been faithful to me all my life. As I have become older and wiser, I truly appreciate all of my blessings.

Before they were born, I worked on documenting our family history so that my grandchildren and beyond would never doubt where they came from. I spent four years researching and documenting Butler family history so that my children would be grounded. I traced our history to the early 1800s in the South. I thought about my unborn children as I drove through the backroads of Calhoun County, South Carolina to see our family's last name on the cornerstone of the local church that was built a long time ago. My children would have a long lineage of strong Black men and women as a strong foundation. Our family has PhDs, entrepreneurs, civil rights activists, and educators. This is now their DNA that God has placed in them to do His Will.

When my wife was pregnant with my first daughter, I was so excited! Before the delivery, I would have to walk my bride all night to help induce her labor. When she finally came, I heard her first cry and gave her her first kiss and hug.

After she was born, my baby wouldn't open her eyes despite the doctor's and my multiple patient attempts. Then my wife Pam softly called, "Christina." It was at that time that my daughter opened her big, beautiful eyes and looked at me. I don't remember anything after that, which leads me to believe I Blacked out. Yes, she had that much of an impact on me.

Christina has her mother's eyes and ability to make me laugh with my laugh-lines when you smile. I call her my mini me because we think alike when it comes to patience with people. Of my three kids, she has always been my mischievous one. Ever since she was a little girl, she would always frustrate me and then make me laugh out loud in her weird way of apologizing. As she has grown into her own, I have seen several God-given gifts and talents that include modeling, liturgical dance, entrepreneurism, and academics.

Christina has her grandparents' passion for activism for African Americans as well as the underprivileged. As a college student, her grandmother participated in "sit-ins" while attending South Carolina State University. Christina attended Benedict College and got the full HBCU experience that she needed to prepare her for this tough world. As a student, she went to the streets of Atlanta to protest the George Floyd assassination. As parents, we were proud yet anxious for her during this critical time in history. As her dad, I know that she will continue to speak for the unspoken. As the Bible says, "Speak up for those who cannot speak for themselves; ensure justice for those being crushed. Yes, speak up for the poor and helpless, and see that they get justice" (Proverbs 31:8–9, NLT).

As a little girl, Christina was called the little prayer warrior. Her prayers were heartfelt and strong. She also participated in liturgical dance as well as several choirs. She attended our local home church for her spiritual covering. It was the fervent prayers of our pastor and congregation that guided our family. The Bible tells us, "Blessed are those who find wisdom, those who gain understanding, for she is more profitable than silver and yields better returns than gold." (Proverbs 3:13–14, NIV).

Family is also very important to Christina. She is very protective of her siblings as well as her mother and father. When I am disobedient to her mother's advice for my health care, she will say, "No worries, I'm on my way, Dad". She keeps me in line. She fully embodies Colossians 3:23-24: "And whatever you do, do it heartily, as to the Lord and not to men, knowing that from the Lord you will receive the reward of the inheritance, for you serve the Lord Christ" (NKJV).

I have watched Christina grow from a fun-loving child to the beautiful, intelligent, independent woman whom everyone still loves. She attracts people with her beauty, inner strength, intelligence, as well as her sense of humor. She has her mother's heart, always wanting to help someone. I am so proud of the achievements that she has made in her life, and I constantly pray for her safety and making the right decisions.

It was February 26, 1995, when I was overwhelmed with God's blessing of a Girl Dad promotion. The first glimpse of her that I remember seeing is a soft "poof," which was all of that thick hair that she had on her head as she crowned during delivery. I yelled, "Pam, here comes the baby!" Then I started sobbing because the new mom's high-arching eyebrows and peek-a-boo eyes appeared in response to my announcement, of which she was clearly aware via labor pains. I cried," Pam, she looks just like you!" My wife then said, "Let me see her." The doctor slightly tapped my baby girl and said, "Crystal." Crystal started crying with a high-pitched song that was simply music to my ears. The second daughter was born safely.

I could not believe that God had blessed me with two angels. I became overwhelmed in thought about all of the things in my past that did not please God, and yet still He blessed me with so much love!

Crystal always wanted to please others and do her best. In the fall play at school, her teacher asked her to stand on one of the floor tiles while she positioned the other students. Crystal dared not to move from that spot no matter how long it took the teacher. Her high energy also was always an asset to her. She had a world-class track career with the local track club, earning her way to the nationals twice. Her coaches knew how to get the max out of her. They would make her mad at them, then she would win first place. This career resulted in many trophies and medals!

There are some aspects of life that you don't get to choose. She is my hero. My baby girl accepted, excelled, and persevered with the diagnosis of type 1 diabetes. She decided to focus on nutrition and strength training to attack this issue.

Her success in this was not a surprise to me because she has always been known as a fighter. She would never back down and would push herself until the challenge was resolved. As a health role model, she continues to encourage others to take better care of their health, and that will be a jewel in the crown in the long run.

Crystal is able to conquer her goals through one of her strongest character traits: discipline. Whether it is academics, sports, or fitness, she will study, focus, and train hard to achieve the goals that sets for herself. Through her persistent patience, if she requires an answer from me, she stands there and waits until I deliver what she requested. When she was accepted at Hampton University with financial aid, she was pleased yet determined that Spelman College would be her home. There were 400 openings for over 4,000 applicants, yet those stifling statistics did not sway her desire. Through academic success and praying without ceasing, Crystal got accepted and graduated on time with honors! As a move of God, her grades were so great as she matriculated as a Spelmanite that her remaining loans were waived.

I continued to pray for my daughter throughout life with the challenges that she was assigned to face so early in her life, and I know she has the favor of God. Whether it is an academic challenge, health concern, relationship, or financial aid, God has come through! I believe that her unwavering faith has made the success that she has had in her life. Today she is a remarkable young lady. Never in my wildest dreams would I have seen the blessings that God has placed in her life. She is a strong, success, driven, and caring person who has not allowed health challenges or relationships break her. As she continues to be all God has called her to be, I know she will continue to manifest the desires of her heart through doctoral studies and entrepreneurship in the health and fitness sector.

It has taken me over twenty-nine years of raising daughters, and they are two of the most precious things with which God has blessed me in my lifetime. It is a privilege and an honor that God has trusted me with his angels on earth.

Raising a daughter is tough, from hair day (whew) to doing my best to comfort them when the monthly cramps occurred. It was difficult when they left me and ventured out because I couldn't be there to protect them. But now I have comfort in knowing that they are His child and He created them with their own purpose.

One of the biggest mistakes that I made in parenting was that I was not able to adequately teach my children about finances. I was never taught about finances, and I had a front row seat to watching my parents struggle financially. I grew up in a middle-class, blue-collar, working family that had just enough means to make it through. I was never taught about savings, investments, and taxes from my parents because they were just attempting to survive. My dad made several unsuccessful attempts to own businesses. However, these businesses never made a major profit. The majority of the income was used to cover the operating expenses. I did not blame my father but was proud that he was doing the best that he could. This would leave my mom struggling to feed her family and keep the lights on. Neither of my parents had a college education to properly prepare them for successfully operating businesses. I had to finance my education through financial aid and jobs. As a teenager and a young man, I did not have the discipline or the knowledge to have businesses, home ownership, and investments to write off for taxes. I had no clue about tax planning, the stock market, and savings.

This lack of knowledge and discipline with money did not allow me to adequately finance college educations or provide down-payments for a house for my children to live in. I am determined, however, to not have my debt passed to them. I will invest in the futures of their children so that they will not have to struggle financially.

But I did get some things right! I invested time, money, and energy ensuring that my daughters know who they are as Black girls. Church is not an option in the Butler household, but a requirement. Whether it was church service, Sunday school, or the church choir, we made sure that our children regularly and consistently attended these events. It was never a question of whether or not they felt like going to church, and they knew not to assert it if they did not feel like going.

My wife and I also encouraged lots of youth activities to include liturgical dance, piano, competitive cheer, track and field, football, basketball, and Girl Scouts. I was a present and active participant. I used to say, "Once the pen hits the check, that is a commitment." That meant the kids would finish it through the end! I taught them about who they were as Butler children and made sure they spent quality time with grandparents, and even their great-grandmother in Sumter, to supplement our family history. My daughters didn't just receive a Christian education, but they also received an HBCU education with Bennett and Spelman Colleges.

I have made mistakes and victories, but God has been there to help me care for His children. The Holy Bible has given me an answer to every aspect of raising girls.

THE CHARGE

As fathers, I hope that you will follow God's Word in raising your precious daughters.

As a Girl Dad, I will make sure that my daughters are taught about Jesus Christ and receive salvation.

As a Girl Dad, I will ensure that they receive the best education possible.

As a Girl Dad, I will support their physical, mental, and spiritual health.

As a Girl Dad, I will remain very knowledgeable about finances, including businesses, home ownership, and investments, so that I can teach and model the expectation.

As a Girl Dad, I will remind them how much they are loved, valued, and appreciated.

As a Girl Dad, I will raise them as non-apologetic, strong, empowered Black women who know who they are.

DEAR DAUGHTER

My Beautiful Black Daughters,

It is my prayer that God develops you into the Godly women that He wants you to be. I declare and decree that God transforms you into the women of God that he is for thought before the earth was even formed. I hope that you develop into the different characteristics of virtuous women. I know this is a charge or a heavy burden to place upon you, but you can only do it by having a strong relationship with God. Even if you don't reach these different characteristics all at once, do not feel bad; you can only attempt to receive characteristics by having a close relationship with Jesus Christ.

One of the first things that I wish that you will work on is the control of your tongue. Matthew 15:11 says it's not what goes into the mouth defiles a person but what comes out of the mouth defiles a person. As you put good things into your body through your mouth, I pray that only good things come out of your mouth.

Many things are impossible unless you have the right heart. The heart is desperately wicked, and you can only have your heart corrected by Christ, who can turn your stony heart to flesh. I pray that you both become women who are after God's own heart. With the heart of God, he will send a "king" to you. This "king" is the type of man whom God has created for both of you. It doesn't make a difference if he was a prodigal son. Which man has not been one? It is where he is now and where he is going. Don't fault him for his past transgressions as you pray for him not to hold yours against you.

Proverbs 31:30 says, "Charm is deceitful, and beauty is vain, but a woman who fears the Lord is to be praised" (NKJV). You have charm and beauty, but I want God to develop the "fear" of the Lord. The fear of the Lord is the reverence of the Lord. Use this as a compass in your heart that will help you navigate this thing called life. I have seen you mom grow over the years into this Titus 2 type of woman of God, so it would make sense that you seek out her wisdom often.

Stay in the presence of God daily. He is there for you always. He has promised to never leave you nor forsake you. This is a promise from God. Even when you are doing wrong, God is there to forgive you if you ask Him. You are no longer following the world, but you are seeking His marvelous Light.

God has such major and awesome plans for you (Jeremiah 29:11), but you have to allow Him to become a major part of your Life in order for it to come to fruition. You are God's children, and know that Satan cannot challenge you without permission from God. He has already provided you with a way of escape from every temptation.

I declare and decree that the Blood of Jesus protects you from low self-esteem, lack of trust, feelings of inferiority, and racism and that no man harms you in any way. I pray to God that you are not in the sight of any pedophile, pornographer, rapist, or robber in the Name of Jesus. I pray for a Godly increase in your finances and business opportunities and that you have a long life.

HEALTHY RELATIONSHIPS START WITH A HEALTHY YOU

I pray that God breaks the hold of unhealthy relationships and creates Godly relationships for you. May He present you with the Godly husbands that he has already created for you. Allow Him to create a new creature in Christ in you to prepare you for the husbands that He has created for you. May you marry and submit to men who submit to God. May you then become fruitful and multiply Godly seeds that will glorify Him. I know that God will heal your hearts from any past heartbreaks by ungodly and immature men. I pray that your relationship and love for your siblings remain unbroken.

KNOW YOUR WORTH

I pray that God reveals to you your value to Him as well as to those around you. Once you realize your value and your worth to God, your self-esteem and confidence will be unlimited. No weapons formed against you shall prosper. Make sure that others know and respect your value. Let no one minimize you. You will not be ignored. You will not be silenced. You have the DNA of generations of strong and outspoken women. God is Hope. As long as there is Jesus Christ, you have a future and a Hope! Therefore, keep the Faith and move on. You serve an excellent God. Therefore, in everything that you do, do it in excellence. Walk in the excellence that is inside of you.

STAY COMMITTED

Let your yes mean yes and your no mean no. God made a commitment to you when His son died on the cross for your sins, so make commitments to God when you are doing His work.

REMAIN FAITHFUL

It is faith and belief that move God. Your parents have faith in you, so continue to allow God to direct your paths. Set personal goals for yourself. Whether it is finances, fitness, ministry, or business, set and reach your goals and visions. Habakkuk 2:2-3 talks about writing the vision and making it plain, for the vision is yet for an appointed time. I can only imagine what God has in store for you. I prophesize a growing company with franchises, a large presence on social media and magazine covers, clothing lines, book deals, blogs, and a successful business. Finally, I see a family that God has made for you coming into your lives.

May God bless you with generations of Godly offspring. I pray that He covers your family in the blood of Jesus. You will become great mothers who will raise Godly children and manage the household. Allow God to send you to church, where you will serve and support the Pastor.

Embrace yourself, your crown of thick hair, your beauty, and who you are as strong yet delicate women. Tap into the vast richness of your vast African heritage. Be celebrated, not tolerated.

You're my Black doll baby.

Chapter 4

PROMOTE PERSEVERANCE

by Gregory Clark

If there were one movie that captures the dynamics of the relationship of a father and his family, for me it would be my favorite: *Fences*. The movie hits home for me. I was raised in a military household with only a brother and no sisters, so I am not ashamed to admit that our household wasn't big on sharing emotions, especially from men. I love my dad with everything in me, so it may catch him by surprise that Denzel Washington's character in the movie *Fences* brings back memories of my youth. For those who have seen the movie, it captures a classic tussle between father and son. Finally, the son asks his dad why he doesn't like him. Without batting an eye, Denzel explains that as a man, he would be best not to worry about someone liking or loving him. Instead, his concern should be that whomever he is dealing with is doing right by him and giving him the respect that he deserves. Now, for the record, I knew that my dad loved me. I can say that with all my heart and soul. We joke and laugh today like we are school-age friends. But as I was growing up, we didn't go around showing many emotions between men. Our love and respect for each other was just something that was understood.

As a father of two daughters, I had to learn that my interaction with my father and what worked to raise men was not necessarily the most appropriate path for raising little girls. In the beginning, this wasn't easy for me to understand. Boys are raised to be tough and can be emotionally disconnected at times. The contrast between how I was raised and the man I needed to become in order to raise my daughters was in many ways stark. However, despite my initial challenges, I was lucky! I had my lovely wife and at various times my mother and mother-in-law to help guide me and soften my stance to ideas that were completely foreign to my understanding. I even had the mentorship of a very accomplished Girl Dad: my father-in law. I am not ashamed to admit that without the counsel of these amazing women and men, I would have made far more mistakes as I navigated my way through my daughters' lives. They taught me the art of listening and communicating and the importance of praying for my little girls, showing me levels of patience that I didn't realize I had within me. For men, things are Black and white, but girls see various shades of gray. We focus on our current circumstances, and girls focus on how you made them feel. Oftentimes, we get so locked in on the "here and now" that we allow our focus to escape what is often more important. We focus on having enough money to take care of necessities while also providing the things our families want that we overlook the simplest things, like love, attention, and communication. It is now that I am older and (hopefully) wiser that I see the importance of the insight that these amazing people shared with me, and I am forever grateful to them for imparting their wisdom upon me.

Like many young men of my community and culture, I decided to start a family well before I developed a plan, or more specifically, secured the financial means to fund any sort of a plan. I became a Girl Dad at the young age of twenty-one, which was actually older than many of my friends but much earlier than the direction intended for my life. While attending Howard University, I met my soulmate and embarked on a love story that has spanned for nearly thirty years and intensifies every day. In the beginning of our love story—I will be 100 percent honest—I didn't know that we would make it, and if I were a betting man, the odds were totally stacked against us. Both being young, my wife and I set sights on what we would do to best raise our daughter. During disagreements, that conversation would sometimes shift to us both leaving school and moving back to our respective homes—her in Los Angeles and me possibly embarking on endeavors of my own back in Georgia. But that scenario never went far because of our love for each other and our desire to give our daughter the best life we could. And throwing in the towel would not allow me to be a full-time father to my oldest daughter, so we both persevered and made a conscious decision to be determined, mature, and responsible parents without the closeness and support of our family. This was much easier said than done. While that sounds admirable and outstanding, we were both naïve and had no idea of the difficulties we would face along the way. Our decision to start a family at such a young age was viewed by family and friends alike as the craziest of ideas, and though we were both too stubborn to admit it, they were absolutely correct in their concerns. We had both just began enjoying our youth—moving to Washington DC to attend "the Mecca" (Howard University). My wife had aspirations of becoming a lawyer, and I had sights on becoming a mogul on Wall Street. We were both too young to be fully prepared for the love we encountered and the realization of how it would alter our plans. Both my wife and I shared those concerns and had no clue if the love we believed we felt for each other would weather the storms that we were sure to encounter by traveling this path. Through my daughters, I realize that we made the best decision, and I am thankful to God that we allowed faith to overshadow our doubts and to move forward to raise amazing children.

Making fatherhood my primary endeavor allowed me to be an integral part of both my daughters' lives and led to my wife of now twenty-six years building a fabulous life for our daughters in the state of Maryland, far from the places we once called home. None of this was easy, but through the grace of God, we were able to remain steadfast in our love and withstand the financial, emotional shortfalls, and struggles with maturity and plans for our futures. When my first daughter was an infant, I can recall being a young college student, working a full-time job at the local YMCA as a Youth Director, and coming home to study with my daughter in my arms. One day, I remember that I had fallen behind on my coursework for a business law course I was taking and approached my instructor for more time to complete the assignment. Without taking the time to hear my full plea, he simply told me that I must "keep moving." I realized in that moment that my decisions were my decisions alone and the world didn't want to hear my excuses. To be a responsible father to my daughter, I had no choice but to keep moving! While my circumstances at the time were not optimal and my finances were tighter than I had ever imagined, I had to make the most of my opportunities and make the appropriate sacrifices to create a better life for my daughter. Based on that motivation, I went on to graduate from Howard University with a degree in finance. If anything is true of osmosis in the formative years of young children, I am certain that my daughter can now recite financial formulas because she was with me along the way and served as a valued study partner and beacon of light to helping me steady my focus and achieve my goal.

After I graduated from college, my second daughter was born. Life for both my wife and me was much easier this time around but far from being ideal. While I was now working a better job and making more money, we now had twice the amount of expenses as we attempted to embark on what we thought was the "American Dream." Because of our upbringing, I wanted my wife to stay home and focus on raising our children. I believed it was incumbent on me to provide what was necessary for my family just as my father and father-in-law did for their families. Despite any financial shortcomings, we made certain that our daughters would never feel the impact of our struggles. We wanted them to have and experience the best and made sure to keep them busy with all sorts of activities. I am proud to say that in their young life they were exposed to a full spectrum of opportunities and extracurricular events. We made sure to place them in various activities including dance, acting, gymnastics, and even video editing and chess—anything to keep their mind firmly rooted. Looking back, I am proud to realize that they were instructed in dance by the multi-talented and amazing Debbie Allen, performed with Alvin Ailey's world-renowned dance company, were the first to perform in DC's rendition of the Chocolate Nutcracker, and even assisted in video editing for BET. As they both got older, we continued to make sure we strategically positioned them for success, ensuring that they explored various opportunities to see life from a different perspective from what they lived. This led to an opportunity to travel and study in Guatemala. We encouraged them to stretch themselves by not just participating in school but placing themselves into challenging programs that would benefit them in the future. My oldest daughter was accepted into both Project Lead the Way, an engineering program, and the Academy of Finance offered by her high school. And our youngest daughter was accepted into the Academy of Health Sciences program in high school, which allowed her to obtain both her high school diploma and an associate's degree on the same day, thus reducing her college education by two years and allowing her to graduate at an early age with her bachelor's degree.

Both of my daughters participated in competitive cheerleading. This required full family participation due to rigid practice, travel, and competition schedules. For a time, we were all traveling up and down the east coast from Florida to Rhode Island for competitions, and I can recall being one of very few dads in attendance. While supporting my daughters in their activities, I gained many adopted daughters in the process, and I am equally proud of them and remain involved in many of their lives today.

For any future or current cheer dads, let me be honest: cheerleading can be one of the most taxing experiences known to man! But watching them practice a routine and seeing them perform is nothing short of remarkable! Having participated in athletics in my youth, I could really see their passion come to life. I gained a lot of respect for my daughters by watching them perform. Cheerleading amplified many of the things I instilled in them, such as being vocal, paying attention to details, and not shying away in the crowd. But what thrilled me most was that I could also see a little of myself in them as they performed. While this was not football or basketball (things in which I participated when I was younger), I could see my passion, determination, and focus exuding from them while going through their performances. It was spectacular watching my little girls thrive under that spotlight with hundreds and sometimes thousands of viewers from competing teams hoping that they miss a somersault, step out of bounds, or fail to show energy. The little things mean a lot! While cheering was my daughters' sport of choice (and yes, I now realize that it is a sport), the point is to become involved with whatever activity your daughter chooses. If she one day wakes up and decides she wants to be the next Patrick Mahones, pull out those old cleats and start running some routes! Your full-fledged participation will speak volumes, and she will realize that you, too, are invested in and supportive of her dreams.

One of my fondest memories of my daughters' childhood occurred at maybe the unlikeliest of moments. We were on vacation in Las Vegas, Nevada, and during our trip, my daughter started her cycle for the very first time. Knowing this was a confusing and awkward time for her, my wife suggested that I run off and get her something special. She was thinking maybe ice cream. If I am being honest, this moment unsettled me maybe more than it did her. My baby was becoming a woman right before my eyes. I felt like I was losing time. My little girl was growing up. In my panic, I set off through Caesar's Palace to find some ice cream. If anyone is ever in this casino, I must admit it is the worst place to find something as simple as an ice cream cone. While I was nowhere close to the ice cream stand, I found, in my disillusionment, something much better—something my daughter would remember forever and long after the ice cream melted down her arm. While passing a Tiffany's store, I walked in and found the perfect gift. I found a nice but simple necklace with a beautiful "girly" charm that would symbolize that day and moment in her life. With the necklace, it was easier to break the ice and let her realize that what she was experiencing was a beautiful moment in womanhood and less a weird, overwhelming, and frightening moment. (Of course, I was the one who was frightened.) Clearly, my gift was over the top, but it captured the moment for the both of us and helped break the ice. To this day, this moment remains a highlight that we will both never forget. While I don't suggest going to Tiffany's to symbolize every moment in your daughters' lives—there will be many, I assure you—what I do suggest is that you make moments memorable. Create memories that you and your daughter/s can sit back and reflect on as you both get older.

As many would agree, one of the biggest challenges for any father is the transition from when daddy is the apple of their daughters' eyes to when they begin to have an interest in boys. If I am transparent, both of my daughters are now mothers, and their scenarios with boys at times have been far from what I would have imagined their relationships would be. As a dad, no guy is ever perfect for your angel. However, I also realize that I was once perceived as that young boy derailing the dreams another father had for his daughter. To overcome that, I had to prove myself and my intentions. I had to show my wife's father that I was mature, respectful, and able to provide for and protect his daughter. I encourage my daughters to invest time in people who share their core values. So, when I notice a deviation from this concept, I do not hesitate to let them know my concerns. Being from the South, I can recall my grandfather saying that "you can wrestle with pigs, but you don't have to stay in the slop." While this advice may seem to be an extreme example to some, it translated to me that we all may find ourselves in unfavorable situations, but it is what you do beyond that point that really matters. When we find ourselves in an unfavorable position, getting there isn't the ultimate failure, but failing to acknowledge a need for change and not dusting yourself off and moving on is the ultimate transgression.

My daughters are both now adults. I look at them today, and I am extremely proud of the exceptional women into whom they have matured. I am often astonished that they are the result of two young, stubborn Howard students who lucked into a romance. Now that they are adults, I realize that the upbringing and many life lessons my wife and I provided for them have not gone unnoticed and were not provided by us in vain. The challenges we overcame to provide for them and create a suitable world for them that they could appreciate and in which they could flourish have taken root. The adage that "you cannot un-ring a bell" is true. By instilling a household full of love, faith, and integrity, I can watch them now as they raise their own children and know that they were paying very close attention to their parents as we were simply figuring it all out. I am extremely proud of my daughters and their many accomplishments because for one, they did not take the easy route. They both challenged themselves and are college educated. They own and operate their own businesses and have even followed in our footsteps as licensed real estate agents in the DC, Maryland, and Virginia (DMV) area. They have learned from our life experiences and have even joined my wife and me to create a legacy that we hope can be passed down to the next generation.

THE CHARGE

As a Girl Dad, I say to those who read my story: keep moving! No one starts this journey with all the answers, so surround yourself with those who can provide meaningful counsel.

As a Girl Dad, I will continuously cover my daughters in fervent prayer and guide them with faith through their journey. I will be active in my daughters' lives and treasure every moment from infancy to adulthood and everything in between. I will create lasting memories on which my daughters can reflect later in life and share a laugh, smile, or maybe a warm hug. I will learn to enjoy the moments and be present in them. I will be supportive and encouraging of my daughters' dreams, and above all, enjoy every single moment of being a Girl Dad!

DEAR DAUGHTER

Dear Daughter,

My little princess, I pray that you will continue to reach for goals that to most will appear unattainable. I pray that you will always realize that you were blessed with an abundance of blessings and that you will never need anyone's validation. I pray that you will value your uniqueness and never conform to another person's vision. I pray that you will seek and discover your passion and dedicate your energies into living a life full of meaning and purpose. And most of all, I pray that you become the best version of *you* that there could ever be.

Chapter 5
PURSUE THE PURPOSE

by Julius Davis

DEVELOPING STRONG CULTURAL IDENTITIES IN BLACK GIRLS

Black girls' and women's identity, image, and character are constantly under attack in popular media, society, and school systems. Many shows and popular media sources depict Black women as angry, violent, materialistic, unintelligent, and promiscuous. The brilliance, multidimensionality, and loving nature of Black women are rarely portrayed in popular media. The beauty and innocence of Black girls are attacked through educational policies that vilify their natural hair and the increasing disciplinary actions taken against them for perceptions about them being loud, aggressive, and disrespectful. Girl Dads must combat the negative attacks against Black girls' identity, image, and character in raising our daughters. As a Girl Dad, I have worked with my wife to build a strong foundation anchored in Black/African history and culture to positively develop my daughter's identity and character as the foundation for who she will become as a Black woman.

As a Black father scholar, I use Kawaida womanism to think about raising my daughter and developing a strong racial, cultural, and gender identity in a world that does not value her innocence, humanity, girlhood, and womanhood (Karenga and Tembo 2012). Kawaida womanism is rooted in Dr. Maulana Karenga's (2008) Kawaida philosophy and practice framework: "an ongoing synthesis of the best of African thought and practice" (p. 3) to achieve liberation for Black people. Kawaida womanism is a part of a larger discourse on Black girls' and women's identities as African and bringing out the best of what it means to be a Black African woman committed to family, community, and the liberation of Black people (Karenga and Tembo 2012). This chapter shares my perspective and approach as a Girl Dad raising a Black girl with a healthy racial, ethnic, cultural, gender, identity, and character to prepare her to commit her education, life, and profession to the liberation of Black people.

MY FAMILY CONTEXT FOR RAISING A BLACK GIRL

My daughter is being raised in a family context with a mother and father who have been married for over ten years and three brothers. As a Girl Dad, raising a daughter is a collaborative process with my wife, but I have my unique perspective as a Black man and father heavily influenced by my worldview.

My wife and I gave my daughter the African name Hakika, which means truth, certainty, and justice. In African tradition, names are important, and it is expected that children will honor their names and live up to their meaning. My wife and I spent a lot of time researching and thinking about names and their significance for our daughter aligned with our African worldview, our knowledge of her, and the vision we have for her life and future.

My daughter is five years old and at the foundational stages of developing her identity as a Black African girl. She is the other half of fraternal twins. Since she was in her mother's womb, my daughter displayed the resilience and tenacity of many Black girls and women I know and admire. I remember the day the doctor told my wife and me that something was wrong with the health of our developing babies. My son was not getting the proper nutrients from the umbilical cord and was not growing properly for his developmental stage. This information about the well-being of our babies was concerning for my wife and me. The silver lining in the news was that my baby girl was doing fine and taking care of her brother in the womb.

My daughter has been a nurturer of her twin brother since they were in the womb. Her nurturing personality has carried over to her older brother, baby brother, and parents. Not only is she a nurturer, but she is also brilliant and determined. I have watched my daughter learn, problem-solve, and establish herself among her brothers. My daughter is committed to learning anything you put in front of her. She will do her best to figure out any challenge put before her on her own. Not only is she smart, but she is beautiful! When I look into my daughter's eyes and stare at her face, I see two of the most important, influential, and beautiful Black women in my life—my wife and mother. I am blessed to have a beautiful, intelligent, and loving daughter.

My daughter is raised in a Pan-African family that values connecting her and her siblings to Africa, Black history, and culture across the diaspora. This approach serves as the foundation for grounding her identity as a Black African girl who will become a strong Black woman. My wife and I are preparing our daughter to contribute to the upliftment and liberation of Black people. My daughter's preparation to be a Black African girl and woman started at conception and continues in our home, our family, and the larger Black community. My wife is the first example of Black African womanhood for my daughter.

My family has been working to reclaim our African heritage and culture and pass that on to my daughter. A few years ago, my wife and I used a Black-owned company specializing in African ancestry to learn more about the specific African countries and tribes from which our family lineage originated. On her maternal side, my wife's African lineage is from Cameroon, and her tribe is Tikar. On her paternal side, her lineage is from Mozambique, and her tribe is Makua. My African lineage is traced back to Guinea-Bissau and the Balanta tribe on my paternal side and Sierra Leone and the Mende and Temne tribes on my maternal side. As a part of our efforts to learn more about our African heritage, we planned to visit the countries and tribes of our family lineage. Before the coronavirus pandemic, our immediate family traveled to Cameroon to learn more about our ancestors, people, and tribe. We met many of our people in the Tikar nation and participated in a traditional ceremony to welcome our family to the village and induct us into the tribe. My daughter has traveled to Cameroon and participated in the ceremony. During the ceremony, she was given a Tikar name by the queen mother of the village. The pandemic has disrupted our family plans to expose my daughter and other children to their African family lineage through travel, but we continue to teach them at home.

My daughter has only attended African-centered educational institutions throughout her short academic career. Before the pandemic, my wife and I traveled from Baltimore, Maryland, to an African-centered school in Washington, DC, to ensure that my daughter and other children received an education grounded in their history and culture. At these schools, my daughter was taught by Black women who self-identified as African and embraced elements of Kawaida womanism or African-centered perspectives. In these educational facilities, the school environment constantly reinforced a love of Black/

African history and culture and positive images of Black people, leaders, and girls and women across the diaspora. My daughter learned African dance from older Black girls and women at her schools and community. To date, she has attended three African-centered educational institutions, and one of the schools had a womanhood preparation program for the Black girls attending the school. She was consistently exposed to a diverse cadre of Black women representative of Black African women's brilliance, multidimensionality, and beauty throughout the diaspora. Most of these schools were led by multi-talented and gifted Black women.

We only celebrate holidays grounded in Black history and culture in my family to help further develop my daughter's identity and commitment to her people. While my family celebrates many holidays anchored in Black history and culture, Umoja Karamu (Anyike 1997) and Kwanzaa (Karenga 1997) are two key holidays used to honor my daughter as a Black girl and woman. Umoja Karamu means unity feast, and it is a holiday founded in 1971 by Dr. Edward Sims, Jr. to commemorate Black life historically, contemporarily, and in the future. The holiday is observed on the fourth Sunday of November, and there are five important periods: 1) Black life before slavery, 2) Black life during slavery, 3) Black life upon emancipation, 4) Black life during the liberation struggle, and 5) Black life in the future. There is a ceremony to pay homage to the creator, family, national ancestors, and elders and presentations of each period before the unity feast. During our family observance of Umoja Karamu, my daughter is actively involved in preparing the feast, and organizing and implementing the ceremony. At my daughter's school, she would participate in the Umoja Karamu program for Black families and the community.

In December, my family celebrates Kwanzaa at home and in many African-centered communities throughout the East Coast. Kwanzaa means "first fruits" and is an international holiday anchored in African harvest celebrations throughout different parts of Africa. Kwanzaa is also anchored in Black history and culture throughout the diaspora. The non-heroic holiday was created in 1966 by Dr. Maulana Karenga. The seven-day holiday is celebrated from December 26 to January 1. There are seven principles for Kwanzaa called the Nguzo Saba: 1) Umoja (unity), 2) Kujichagulia (self-determination), 3) Ujima (collective work and responsibility), 4) Ujamaa (cooperative economics), 5) Nia (purpose), 6) Kuumba (creativity), and 7) Imani (faith). There is a description that explains each principle and that is used for each day of the holiday. My daughter is actively involved in setting up the Kwanzaa altar, decorating our home, planning activities, and cooking the feast. My daughter also performs African drumming and dances, plays, and other creative acts with peers at her school during Kwanzaa for Black families and the community. As a family, before the pandemic, we attended community Kwanzaa events hosted by Black organizations committed to the liberation and upliftment of Black people in Philadelphia,

Pennsylvania; Washington, DC; Richmond, Virginia; and different cities and counties in Maryland.

MY UNIQUE PERSPECTIVE AS A GIRL DAD

My perspective as a Girl Dad is grounded in my upbringing, my relationship with my grandad and my dad, my African worldview and political ideology, and my commitment to Black people. Throughout my childhood, my father used to tell me, "Know your history." As a young man, I did not know what he meant, but my father's words sent me on a journey to learn more about Black history and culture. This journey led me to develop a Pan-African view of the world and a greater appreciation for who I am as a Black man, father, and scholar raising a Black girl to be a Black woman. I have spent most of my life and educational career learning more about Black history and culture across the diaspora, and now it is a central part of how I raise my daughter and see the world.

My paternal grandfather and grandmother played a significant role during my childhood in grounding my views of Black manhood, fatherhood, and family and how I raise my daughter. My mother and father were teenage parents who instilled many great values and work ethic in me, but I did not benefit from having both of my parents in the household to learn how to function as husband and wife to raise children. Given that my mother and father were teenage parents, my paternal grandfather and grandmother were the first married couple I examined in detail, which taught me the value of family. On Saturdays, when I went to my grandparents' house to work with my grandfather and spend time with them, we always ended the day by going to the grocery store as a family to buy me some food before they dropped me off home. Spending time with my grandparents taught me what it felt like to receive love in a family with both parents. Thinking about those moments as a Girl Dad, I always work to create moments with my daughter to help her understand the importance of love in a family and between a husband and wife. For example, sometimes, I send love messages to my wife through my daughter to express my love to my wife, and those moments also allow me to express love to my daughter.

My grandfather and father taught me the importance of discipline, taking care of my responsibilities, providing for my family, and being confident in who I am as a Black man and father. As a Girl Dad, I constantly work to teach my daughter those lessons and the important values I learned from my dad and grandad. My father and grandfather are two of the most confident Black men that I know and two of the best fathers I know. They taught their daughters and sons valuable lessons about life, education, wealth building, hard work, Black history, serving your family and community, and having a relationship with the creator. Those lessons I learned from them are all lessons that I work to teach my daughter. Because of my father and grandfather, I see my role as a Girl Dad to teach my daughter valuable lessons that will prepare her for life and develop into a great Black woman like my aunts.

Haki Madhubuti (1996) wrote "A Father's Pledge," which plays a significant role in seeing myself as a father in general and a Girl Dad. The pledge asks fathers to commit daily to being the best father they can be for their children by studying, listening, observing, and learning from mistakes. It asks fathers to openly display love to their wife and children, hug and kiss them, support them, and spend quality time with them. I compliment my daughter on her brilliance, kindheartedness, and beauty regularly. The pledge asks fathers to teach by example, introduce children to something new and developmental each week, be involved in their education and extracurricular activities, and challenge them to do their best. It asks fathers to commit to reading with their children, exposing them to the arts, and organizing family excursions. My daughter and I attend community events that uplift Black families, women, and the larger Black community together. He also stresses the importance of connecting your children to their families. I have fully embraced Madhubuti's pledge and guidance to create a culturally grounded home that represents the best of Black history, culture, and struggle. His pledge expresses the importance of teaching children the importance of being hardworking, responsible, disciplined, fair, and honest. He also stresses the importance of teaching children about the importance of the Black community, political involvement, and economics. I teach her about Black wealth building through our family businesses, investments, and jobs. Madhubuti's pledge has been instrumental in my quest to provide my daughter and larger family with an environment to develop into a sane, loving, productive, spiritual, and hardworking Black woman who will make an important contribution to the upliftment and liberation of her people.

As a Girl Dad, I want my daughter to commit her education, time, resources, gifts, and talents to the upliftment and liberation of Black people, and I regularly work to set an example for her to know to do so. I regularly buy my daughter books that feature positive Black families, girls and women, history, and culture. As a Black man, father, and scholar, I have committed my education and life to the upliftment and liberation of Black people across the diaspora. I spend a significant amount of my time and energy developing and implementing programs to uplift the Black community in my personal and professional life. Before the pandemic, my daughter was actively involved in my work to serve the Black community. As a Black male college professor, most of my scholarship, research, teaching, and service focuses on the Black community, emphasizing race, racism, culture, liberation and Black boys and men in education. Teaching my daughter to uplift and liberate Black people is more important to me than her going to college. Woodson (2010) argues that "The large majority of the Negroes who have put on the finishing touches of our best colleges are all but worthless in the development of their people" (p.24). I do not use this quote to disrespect Black people with degrees. Rather, I use it to note that colleges were not designed to prepare Black people to advance their people but build white institutions. From my experiences, most of what I have learned to uplift and liberate Black people did not happen in classrooms. I learned how to do it by studying Black history, culture, civilizations, and leaders on my own and with likeminded Black people and by doing real work to improve Black people's collective conditions. I use my experiences and knowledge to teach my daughter how to uplift the Black community and work towards our collective liberation.

THE CHARGE

As Girl Dads, it is part of our responsibility to help our daughters develop a strong identity as Black girls and women. We live in a society, and most of our daughters attend schools that do not value their humanity, beauty, intellect, gifts, talents, beauty, history, culture, or identity. As Girl Dads, we must work to develop our daughters' identities in accordance with our beliefs and worldview. Our daughters must be prepared to combat the negative images and personal character portrayed in the media of Black girls and women. In my view, the preparation starts at home and continues at the educational and communal institutions and with the Black people with whom we raise our daughters within Black communities. I also think that our daughters' identities, character, and image of themselves must be anchored in Black history and culture, Black holidays, the names we give them, and how they conduct themselves. Black women who were not reared or taught about their history and culture must do the important work of learning it for themselves and aligning with Black people they trust, especially Black women who embrace Kawaida womanism or an African-centered worldview and perspective. Black girls become Black women who determine the future of our Black nation, and we need them to be healthy, grounded, and committed to Black history and culture and our collective liberation.

DEAR DAUGHTER

My message to Black girls and women is that you must decide if you want to commit yourself to the liberation of Black people. No one can make that decision for you because you must be okay with the responsibilities associated with your commitment. My daughter must make the decision for herself too. You stand on the shoulders of many Black girls and women ancestors in your family and the larger Black community who committed to making life better for you and future generations of Black girls and women and the Black family and community as a whole. You must decide whether you will honor their commitment and legacy and make a commitment yourself to learn more about Black history and culture, Kawaida womanism, African-centered perspectives of womanhood, and Black liberation to determine where you are going to contribute. Black girls and women are an integral part of any effort to liberate the Black community. My sister, what will you decide to do? We need your brilliance, gifts, talents, persistence, and resilience to create a Black nation that will support our people. Ase!

REFERENCES

Anyike, J. C. (1997). *African American Holidays*. Indianapolis: Popular Truth Publishing.

Karenga, M. (1980). *Kawaida Theory: An Introductory Outline*. Los Angeles: Saidi Publications.

Karenga, M. (1998). *Kwanzaa: A Celebration of Family, Community and Culture*. Los Angeles: University of Sankore Press.

Karenga, T., & Tembo, C. (2012). Kawaida Womanism: African ways of being woman in the world. Western Journal of Black Studies, 36(1), 33-47. Retrieved from https://www.proquest.com/scholarly-journals/kawaida-womanism-african-ways-being-woman-world/docview/1018074462/se-2?accountid=9683.

Madhubuti, H. (1996). A Father's Pledge. https://thefamilymeeting.wordpress.com/2012/04/01/a-fathers-pledge-by-haki-r-madhubuti/.

Woodson, C. G. (2010). *The Miseducation of the Negro*. Africa World Press.

Chapter 6
PREPARE TO SMILE

by Joseph C. Bryant

According to my mother and older sister, I never smiled much as a child. My early childhood photos prove their claim. I wasn't an unhappy child, though. I got neither too high nor too low about anything. "Phlegmatic" and "even keeled" are a couple words my mother would often use to describe me. Christmases were at times torturous for my parents, who would purchase amazing gifts only for me to respond with a bland "thanks." In other words, no one ever had to tell me to "calm down."

The word "thanks" would come back to bite me a few times through interactions with my daughters. One day, I saw my youngest daughter walking toward me. This was the interaction: Me: "Joey, you're the best!" I said with a big smile. While looking straight ahead, she replied, "Thanks. Don't use the downstairs bathroom. I just pooped."

Not once did she break stride. When sending my oldest daughter out the door for school, I always say, "Have a great day, I love you!" I normally hear back a very bland and plain "thanks." Now I know what you're thinking. "Does that make you want to go back to bed and cry yourself to sleep?" Sometimes, but I normally just go work out and drink some coffee.

My wife, Tenisha, and I have two daughters, Norah, 13 and Johannah (Joey), 9, and a son Quentin, 7. Joey is very affectionate and playful while Norah is inquisitive and enjoys her space. Joey loves dolls, Play-Doh, and being comfy. Norah loves her best friend/stuffed bear, Peter, the color Black, and drawing anime style figures. Over the years, I've learned to greet my children with a smile and always tell them that I love them. It has built trust between us so when situations get difficult, they know things will eventually be okay. Their unique personalities have made my life very eventful.

Their differing personalities on full display occurred about three years ago when I had emergency eye surgery. January 31, 2019, I arrived at my optometrist for an appointment due to a change of vision in my left eye. After less than five minutes into the examination, it was determined that my retina was detached. Either this was the worst upsell of all time or I was in serious trouble.

In a span of three hours, three doctors told me the following:

1. Contact lens specialist: "You probably need emergency surgery to save your eye."

2. Retinal specialist: "You need emergency surgery to repair your detached retina, if not today then certainly tomorrow."

3. Retinal surgeon: "I'll be performing your surgery tomorrow."

Those three doctors saved my eye when I thought I needed a new prescription. That's like going to a mechanic for an oil change and finding out that your battery is dead or going grocery shopping and your bank account is in the negative (both are true stories). Your whole day is changed, you have a ton of phone calls to make, and you're trying to figure out how this is not your fault.

During my recovery at home, Joey nurtured and cared for me, yet her honesty could not be contained. Joey would say things like "How do you feel?" "Do you need anything?" "Can I get you some water?" "Let me see how your eye is doing. Oh, never mind, that's gross, you can cover it up now." Norah looked at me like an exhibit at a freak show. "Now here lying face down on the basement sofa is a very particular creature. You can tell by his moans that he is in incredible pain. Please look (if you can) at the *one-eyed dad monster!*" Norah would say, "Dad, can I see?" "That's cool. Does it hurt?" "Can I touch it?" "Can you shoot lasers out of it?" "Can you see through walls?" "Anyway, hope you get better, bye."

Joey finds joy through sharing, serving, and helping. If she has three pieces of candy, you can guarantee she's giving away at least one of them. That's an incredible feat when you consider that once for a school assignment, she was asked to write in her favorite subject. She said lunch. She meant that more than anything. Norah finds joy in stimulating conversations and exploring new ideas and concepts. We've explored questions like, "Why don't more people walk around with their favorite stuffed animal?" "Is Minnesota known for having great mints and soda?" and "Why aren't pickles considered vegetables?"

One of my favorite things to do is cooking dinner for my family. It's my nightly love letter to them. Through my meals, I'm expressing that I want the best for them, and nothing is better than my food. Even a bowl of cereal is made with love. I also enjoy the solitude that comes with being in the kitchen. It's my happy place. I love the peace, the planning, the multitasking, and the smile from their faces as I watch them eat while pretending to wash the dishes. I love cooking for them! I love the excitement on their faces once I tell them what's for dinner. If chicken or tacos are involved, I'm king for at least a few hours. Even if it's a meal for myself, they love to be my taste testers (whether I ask them or not).

What I didn't realize was that not only did the girls enjoy my food, but they also wanted to join me in my happy place.

More and more, they would ask to cook with me. Initially, I often said, "No, dear. I got it. Maybe another time." But they were persistent, and little by little, I let them in the kitchen, helping here and there. Occasionally, I would let them pick the seasoning for the chicken wings. Lemon pepper is typically chosen. Then, after some time, they were doing more and more with me. After they're done contributing, they always say, "Thanks, dad" and leave with a big smile on their face. Just like their personalities, their own stories are unique. The phlegmatism highlighted by my mother years ago would serve me well through chaos.

NORAH'S FIRST PICTURE DAY

In our townhouse basement, the walls are decorated with paintings of Michael Jordan, Stevie Wonder, and Biggie Smalls as well as several pictures of friends and family. What do you expect from a matrimony made by music? The children occupy most of the walls' very limited real estate. My favorite picture is of Norah when she was four years old. It's the picture I turn to whenever I'm in a random parking lot after an argument with her wondering, "Does she even like me anymore?" I later remind myself, "She doesn't hate you, she's just thirteen. She hates everyone."

When my wife, Tenisha, was pregnant with Joey, I naturally assumed a bigger role when it came to cleaning, cooking, and walking Norah to and from daycare. Though when it came to Norah's clothes and hair, Tenisha never wavered. She was very precise with every braid, twist, and part. Her hairstyles were gorgeous. My role at that time was to ease any stress and lighten her load as much as possible. Everything was going well . . . until picture day.

Sparing the details, my wife woke up very sick one morning, which wasn't uncommon around that time. What made this day different was that Norah's hair needed to be done, her clothes needed to be picked out, and it was her very *first* picture day. My wife could barely move, let alone do a four-year-old's hair. I reassured her by saying, "I got it. No problem. Just rest." I walked out of the room externally confident, yet internally, I was falling apart. "I don't know how to *do* hair; she'll be lucky if her clothes match." What I did know was that I had to move fast. 7:15 am, I had to be on my way to work, so after picking out her clothes (which did match), we went to the bathroom. I got some grease and a pick, and I got busy. "Isn't mommy gonna do my hair?" she asked. "Not today, babe. I got it," I replied. I still think she was fly that day. Wardrobe check: Jean shorts; white shirt with multi-color polka dots; red, white, and blue headband; and the dopest Afro you have ever seen! Picked to perfection! To this day, it was to be one of my finest moments.

Her smile in that photo was incredible. A co-worker saw that picture on my desk one day and said that even her eyes were giving a smile. I have a working theory that Norah's smile in that photo wasn't the normal "one, two, three, cheese" that the photographer famously directs young children to do. She meant to show her teeth on this day. Norah has never faked a smile, a tear, not even a damn cough. She left the house with confidence that day, and it showed in that photo. The chaos of the morning didn't change how she felt about herself. The chaos didn't change what she saw in the mirror. She loved how she looked that day.

For further evidence that the joy shown that day was genuine, year by year, her smile for picture day photos has waned and her eyes haven't quite been the same. Nor should they. Life gets increasingly complicated, and no one is protected from that. Her photographs now represent that growth and complexity. I love and celebrate the young person she is, but I'll always cherish her first picture day. I hope she was thinking of me as she smiled.

But to be honest, she was probably thinking about her stuffed buddy, Peter.

LATE NIGHTS AND EARLY MORNINGS WITH JOEY

In late 2015, I got a new job, which required my family to temporarily move into my parents' basement for a year and a half. This move put us in a position to buy a home and reduced my wife's and my commute time greatly. Those first few months were rough on the children. The basement was small but livable. From the basement, my mother operated her daycare for about fifteen years and retired from it five years prior. Even after we moved in, it still looked like a bunch of toddlers were coming at any moment for circle time and snacks. We converted my mother's old office, located in the rear of the basement, into a bedroom for the children. Because of the rapid changes, the move put a lot of stress on us, and we *all* got sick with colds, sore throats, and pink eye. Have you ever heard of hand, foot, and mouth disease? Spoiler alert: it's trash.

Many nights were spent in urgent care waiting hours to be seen for what normally turns out to be a ten-minute visit just be told to wait in line for a prescription and come back if it gets worse. A trip to urgent care is never pleasant. Everyone is tired and uncomfortable. One night, it was my turn to take our sick child to see the doctor. I always hated when my children got sick, but with Joey, it was especially troubling. She's the heart and soul of the family, the life of the party, and the one that makes us all laugh. When she's sick, you can really see the difference in her spirit. It's as if someone took the engine out of a Ferrari. We were in the lobby waiting with the rest of Prince George's County, and Johannah was drained of her usually abundant energy, scared, and on the verge of tears. This in itself was a rarity due to her remarkable resilience.

To give some context on Johannah, here's a quick story. I don't think Joey has ever had a baby tooth "fall out." Recently, while eating dinner, Joey stopped eating, turned to me, and said the following: "Dad, my tooth is wiggling. I gotta go take it out." The first time Johannah yanked out her tooth, I was horrified. Now, I understand it to be a necessary evil. Since the age of five, as soon as a tooth begins to give way, she becomes the youngest dentist in the world and performs a quick procedure with no parental assistance. When questioned about it, she says, "Of course I took it out, I want the money [from the tooth fairy]!" After cleaning up, Johannah Bryant, D.D.S. in training calmly sat down and finished her quesadilla like nothing happened. To summarize, it takes a lot to rattle her cage.

Options for entertainment were minimal. Even if she brought a toy, she wouldn't have had the energy to play. Joey wasn't complaining, but her labored movements and red-hot skin had me on edge. While externally maintaining my composure and reassuring my daughter, internally I was a wreck. Though the move would prove to be beneficial for our family, my children's health suffered in the short term. I felt so guilty. All I wanted to do in that moment was say I'm sorry. However, at that time, my two-year old would've only responded to, "Let's go home." I just wanted to make her smile, so I did the only thing I could: play music from my phone. Normally, in the mornings, I'd play music for the children as we were getting ready for the day. Joey would always dance, smile, and sing along, so I knew I had a chance to turn things around. I figured, let's have our own private "Silent Party."

I untangled my headphones, placed one earbud in Johannah's left ear and one in my right, and pressed play. I searched until I found something worthy of her approval. Once I did, we listened to that song at least 171 times in a row. She gave me a gentle nudge on the leg whenever something was to be repeated. It was a pleasant distraction for both of us. The smile began to creep along. Though physically ill, she was emotionally on her way back to normal. Soon after, her name was called. We saw the doctor, got the medicine, and went home. After our marathon evening, Joey recovered in a day or two. I was relieved when she started running and jumping in places that she shouldn't again. My guilt would later subside because I realized my wife and I were doing the right thing. For our family to thrive, we all had to be slightly uncomfortable for a while.

Looking back at those moments can be extremely difficult at first. But then I realized those moments needed to happen for us to grow as a family. My daughter's physical growth, on the other hand, is out of control. One day, they're asking you to lift them in the air and spin them around, then the next moment they're looking at you eye to eye demanding more fruit cups. I ask them all the time to stop growing and let me just hold on to these moments. They refuse without even trying. And they're right. Children aren't time capsules, and they cannot be frozen in time. Because of this, I try to enjoy every moment.

Chaos is unforgiving, random, and unpredictable. Being a Girl Dad, I've learned that love is intentional and consistent. Any actions that involve my family are made with that same intentionality and consistency. Through all our chaotic moments, my love for my girls has navigated us through difficult times. It's beautiful to watch them guide each other through their own moments of chaos. If Joey is struggling with her homework, Norah will volunteer to help and will lead her through. If Norah is upset or sad, Joey will spend time with her (whether Norah wants her to or not) and ask her to have a dance party or play a game. They use their gifts to aid each other, and that's the dream scenario for a parent. I can't wait to see who they become as women.

THE CHARGE

As a Girl Dad, I will fail. From my failure, I will learn and grow. When I fail, I will apologize and do better. I don't posture myself as a perfect father but as one who is committed to learning from my mistakes and applying what I learned from them. My daughters deserve that from me.

Norah, I promise to give you all my shirts and hoodies as soon as I'm no longer cool enough to wear them. Johannah, I grant you permission to wear my shoes after my plantar fasciitis sets in. To you both, I am always available to do your hair or have a "silent party" with you in urgent care.

DEAR DAUGHTER

Daughters, I pray that you will always be yourself. Yes, that is far easier said than done and yes, I understand the cost of individuality, but it's necessary in order for you to not only know yourself but to love yourself. Never let the world tell you who you are. They'll always be wrong. I pray that you learn to forgive with the understanding that it sometimes means moving on from something or someone. And I pray that you are accountable for your actions regardless of the outcome. Pride should never stop you from doing what is right. I loved you before I first saw you. May God continue to bless you.

Chapter 7
PIVOT INTO POSITION

by Philip McNair

Black fathers are faced with many unique challenges raising their children, particularly their daughters. What experiences are there to go off of unless raised in a household surrounded by at least one woman? It's also a well-known fact that Black children are less likely to be raised in a two-parent household, and so we tend to miss out on the opportunity of being nurtured by either our mother or father. Most commonly, it's the latter.

While I've cultivated a relationship with my dad as I've gotten older, we lived in two diffcrent states after he and my mom divorced, and so he was not around regularly during my childhood. So, what influences impact our ability to raise our daughters effectively without any firsthand examples of how to actually do it? What tools can Black men equip themselves with to become better fathers of their own? These are just a few thoughts that come to mind regarding the challenges of being a Black Girl Dad.

My journey to becoming a Girl Dad began in the fall of 2004. I didn't have the best grades coming out of high school, and so my options were limited. It was either St. Paul's College, a small HBCU in Lawrenceville, VA, or Hudson Valley Community College in Troy, NY. I decided to stay closer to home trusting that I would improve my grades enough so that I could transfer to a school of my choice. One afternoon, as I was leaving football practice with a few of my friends/teammates, we decided to make a pitstop at the library on campus. There was a beautiful dark-skinned woman whom even my friends noticed sitting all alone at the computer. However, none of them quite had the courage to approach her, and so I decided I'd be the brave one and introduce myself. She told me her name was Tara. We spoke briefly, and then we exchanged telephone numbers.

Shortly after, I decided to give her a call. Our conversation began like any other conversation a teenager would have when getting to know someone. "How old are you? Where are you from? What is your favorite color?" and so on. What I gathered from Tara was that we shared a lot of similarities. Particularly, she was originally from Queens, NY, and her family had since relocated to Albany, NY. Likewise, I had moved from Brooklyn, NY, to Middletown, NY, where I would ultimately finish my high school career.

Tara was a couple of years older than me. At that time, I was eighteen years old and she was twenty years old. She had a son named Tyliek who was four years old and was living with her full time. As a teenager fresh out of high school, I was kind of intrigued by the thought of dating someone I considered at that time to be a "grown woman." Looking back at it, I realize my perception of a real woman was not reality. In addition to taking classes, Tara had a job and even had her own apartment off campus. One thing led to another, and before you knew it, we were dating and in a relationship. Things started off rather fast, but they also felt right at the time.

Before meeting Tara, I would take days off from school at my own discretion, but now that I was spending so much time off campus, my attendance and academic performance declined significantly—so much that people in my dormitory noticed my absence and my room was burglarized of some valuable belongings. Over the next few months, Tara and I would continue enjoying our time together, which mostly included hanging out with her family and friends.

However, in February and March 2005, things would take a turn as Tara informed me that she was pregnant. By this time, I had just turned nineteen years old and was less than a year out of high school. I was in shock and didn't know how I was going to break the news to my mother, Karen. I took the day to process everything that was happening and decided I would let my mother know later that day. I still remember the anxiety I felt when I dialed her number. Anyone who knows my mother can attest that she always has a positive and charismatic attitude. She's my mother, so I know that's not *always* the case, especially being a hard-headed kid growing up in New York.

When she picked up the phone, she was excited to hear my voice and like any other time, asked me how I was doing. I didn't waste time with small talk though. Rather, I broke the news with confidence and without hesitation. "Mom, Tara is pregnant, and I'm going to be a dad." Her reaction was . . . let's just say she was not expecting that call at all. I reiterated that I would be a father, and an active and present one at that. It took some time for the shock to wear off, but once it did, my mother was just as excited as I was. Over the next few months, she would host the baby shower at her home, and we would receive many gifts we would not have been able to afford otherwise.

During Tara's third and final trimester, I found myself preparing to become a father at the tender age of nineteen years old. It was really happening. At this point, I was working part time for Fastenal, a fastener distributor company. My boss, Spencer, understood that at any moment, I would need to leave work at the drop of a dime. I remember the call like it was yesterday; Tara was dilating, and I was advised that she would likely go into labor soon. I called my mother, and she immediately got on the road to drive north to Albany. As I arrived at St. Peter's Hospital, I was filled with excitement standing by Tara's bedside. I watched her push and push until my daughter, Alana Love McNair, came into this world at 7:06 pm on November 29, 2005. I was now officially a Girl Dad!

By this time, I had unenrolled at Hudson Valley Community College and began working full time at a nearby bread factory overnight. On my off days, I would take the night shift caring for Alana so that Tara could get some rest. This routine went on for months and, I must admit, became very challenging over time.

Being a parent requires a lot of sacrifice. While my friends were out enjoying their youthfulness, I was either at work or at home caring for my daughter. Nevertheless, I have some amazing memories from being a new and young Girl Dad. What I didn't know is that being a dad required me to have my cosmetology license. Before leaving the house, I had to find new and creative ways to put her small amount of hair into a ponytail. Nonetheless, I wouldn't change a thing. Those little moments were the start of the bond we share today.

As Alana began to grow into a young toddler, I was there to witness her take her first steps and speak her first words. Once she knew how to walk, it seemed as though she would follow me everywhere. I loved every minute of seeing her blossom before my eyes.

In the beginning of 2007, Tara would inform me that she was pregnant again with my son, Philip, Jr., and so in June 2007, I would make a major life decision to join the United States

Navy. I wanted more for myself and felt the military could help me better provide for my family. While I accomplished some great achievements, I spent a lot of time out at sea and away from my family. I understood the importance of being physically present for your children, and so in 2012, I made the ultimate decision to transition back into the civilian sector.

Unfortunately, by this time, Tara and I had decided to part ways. I must admit, things were rather challenging at first, but we've grown past our misunderstandings and now have a stable coparenting relationship with little conflict. We communicate easily, respect each other, remain flexible to schedules, and most importantly, prioritize the wellbeing of our children. Yet, it is still sometimes difficult to manage the dynamic of raising children in two separate households, especially when the parents have two different parenting styles. At the time of our separation, Alana was too young to understand what was going on. However, our ability to maintain a healthy co-parenting relationship has likely benefited her in many ways. To some extent, our lives have changed for the better. Relationships don't always work out the way you'd expect them to, but despite our differences, we're still able to come together to achieve a common goal.

In an article titled, "How Positive Co-Parenting Produces Mentally Healthy Kids," the writer suggests that perceived coparenting experiences during childhood are likely to be repeated if the child becomes a parent themselves. This is extremely important to me because I do not want my daughter to raise her children in a broken household.

Alana is currently sixteen years old and is growing into an amazing young lady. With a snap of a finger, you realize that one day you're holding your child in one arm, and the next day you're talking to them about boys. Speaking of which, Alana's mother and I have had several sit-down conversations with her regarding her handling of healthy relationships with the opposite sex, things she needs to look out for, how she should conduct herself, and the importance of confidence in herself so that she knows what she should accept and what she shouldn't.

Over the past year, I've had separate conversations with Alana about seeing boys her age. She even spoke to me about a young man whom I had the pleasure of meeting. Surprisingly, our introduction came after he expressed an interest in meeting me. I was a bit taken aback by the gesture, but he seemed to be respectful and well-mannered. During our discussion, I expressed what my rules were for seeing my daughter and what a platonic relationship between teenagers should look like. I explained to them both that they have a lot of life ahead of them and that they should not get too emotionally invested. From my experience, it never ends well to get too emotionally invested. As a teenager, it's difficult to process heartache, and it will cause you to lose focus on other important areas of your life.

In the weeks to follow, Alana and her friend would spend more time together under my supervision. One outing included a trip to Top Golf while I sat at the bar. As a father, it's very important that I support her growth and development. Part of that includes helping her to understand the importance of establishing healthy boundaries in platonic relationships with the opposite sex. Good friends are there to provide emotional support, promote healthy living, and are even there to help you get through difficult times. Personally, I don't know where I would be had I not been surrounded by the female friends that I have in my life.

What I've learned from fathering a teenage girl in 2020 and beyond is that times are much different than they were when I was her age. Social media has such a big influence on how children view the world. It seems that we have to parent them in the real world and also in the digital world. As fathers, we must maintain a healthy balance between allowing our daughters to experience the joys of being a teenager while protecting them from the harmful things this world sometimes has to offer. With that said, it's extremely important for us to talk to our children, ask questions, and stay engaged. A father/daughter bond is special, and it is my responsibility to foster that relationship for as long as I'm around.

I was once told as a young father starting off that my job was not so much teaching her how to be a lady but rather showing her how a lady should be treated; those words have stuck with me till this day. As a father, I also pride myself on being able to protect and provide for my daughter. There is no better feeling than her knowing that she can count on me to be there when she needs me. It's important to note that we as fathers cannot do it all by ourselves. It takes a village to raise a child, and so having positive influences in her life have been invaluable and such a major asset to the both of us. Alana is surrounded by a loving family who cares deeply about her growth and development. She has even been fortunate enough to have a relationship with her great-grandmother, which not everyone is able to experience.

During conversations about life after high school, I've been able to help her future career decision making process by connecting her with people in her fields of interest. While she's changed her mind several times, I try to help her navigate her thought process as best I can. My hope is that by providing her with the tools and resources to make sound decisions, she will have a much smoother transition into adulthood than I did.

Alana has never been much into sports, but I encourage her to stay active and maintain a healthy lifestyle. And while health is usually associated with diet and exercise, I also try to stress the importance of mental health and feeling comfortable enough to talk to someone when you're not feeling your best. Teenagers these days love to lock themselves in their rooms, and so I make it a point to get her out the house, even if it's just for a walk around the neighborhood or a drive around town.

As parents, we all lead busy lives, and so it's sometimes the little things like eating dinner together and asking questions about how things are going. It's important to note that feedback should be bilateral. In the past, I've asked my daughter, "What are some things that you wish I did differently as a father?" It's important that your children understand that there are no restrictions and that they should feel free to answer without the fear of repercussions or backlash. You'll be surprised at the things that are communicated with you in this type of forum. The goal is twofold; first, you want your children to feel comfortable talking to you about anything, and secondly, you want to know what you can do differently to improve your relationship with your children.

Eventually, Alana will go on to graduate high school and be off to the next phase in her life, which will likely be college. She'll make plenty of mistakes along the way, and she'll have to "figure it out" as we all once had to do. Regardless of what mistakes she makes in life, I want her to know that the love her father has for her is without limits.

I understand from my own experience how important it is to have a solid foundation. During my childhood years, I grew up in the church and began to establish a relationship with Christ early on. My mother instilled in me the value of staying connected spiritually because in difficult times, that is sometimes all you have to lean on. While Alana's mother and I share two separate beliefs, I think it's important for her to also build a strong relationship with God. Regardless of the mistakes you make in life, God loves you unconditionally.

So, as my story comes to an end, my hope is that you're leaving inspired.

THE CHARGE

As a Girl Dad, I will always keep God first because without Him, nothing is possible. I won't always get it right, but I will do my best and learn from my shortcomings. I will surround my daughter with love and put her in situations to win. I will be present and involved in every stage of her life. I challenge everyone reading these words to be devoted to fatherhood in each of these ways. Do not be afraid to ask for help. There are a variety of support groups available through local churches and friends and family members who may have dealt with similar experiences of being a Girl Dad.

DEAR DAUGHTER

Dear Daughter,

I'm so proud of the young lady you are today. The mere fact that you're reading this validates that you serve a purpose here on earth. There's only one of you in this entire world, and you should never forget how beautifully and wonderfully made you are.

In life, there will be challenges, but there's a Heavenly Father who does not want to see you fail. Remember, prayer is just a conversation with God, and so talk to Him often. Accept your past without regrets, handle your present with confidence, and face your future without fear.

Don't let the outward world define who you are. You are enough. Be kind to people and generous with your talents. Don't be afraid to love or to be loved. To share your weakness is to make yourself vulnerable, and to make yourself vulnerable is to show your strength. I'll be here to cheer you on.

Signed,
Your Biggest Fan

Chapter 8
PRESSURE COOKER

by Reginald Mack

Before I even begin to get into the meat and potatoes, I have to say thank you to my mother and father for sharing in such a love that produced me, the baby boy of three wonderful children. Their lifelong marriage of over fifty years is something that continues to give me hope for better days ahead. During the publication of this work, my mother received her wings, so Ma, this is dedicated to you.

Hey dads and dads-to-be. I hope all is well as you continue on your journey of life. Life reminds me of an everlasting ongoing obstacle course. One of my partners has the best slogans for her clothing company, "DOPE," which stands for Daily Obstacles Produce Excellence. And right now, it feels like I'm facing every obstacle known to man. I know I'm not the only one who feels this way, but the more we go through, the better we can become if we never give up. No matter how hard it may get, I have to remind myself that success does not come without failure. It's just that I'm at the stage where I feel like I have fallen flat on my face and am slowly beginning to pick myself up off the mat like a boxer who got hit with a devastating blow. Reality is this: sometimes you are going to have to lose in order to win. It may not add up now, but it will. The most important thing is to always remember to take care of yourself so that you can better help and serve others. I believe that is our ultimate mission. I think that the more we do for others, then more will come to us in return. I didn't always think like this. To be honest, as I'm writing, I'm also training myself to think and act more like a king. We speak things into existence, so I won't allow negative thoughts to consume my energy. Life is too short for that. The laws of nature, also known as karma, are very real.

There were times when I was all about me, myself, and I. What others thought of me didn't matter. I was not concerned about "if you do dirt, you get dirt." I knew of the word karma, but I didn't pay it any attention in my younger years. Now I'm forty-three years old, and while I continue to navigate through my journey, things are changing dramatically. What once was considered to be love is now bitter and sorrow. What was comfortable is no longer comfort, and I'm learning a lot as I continue to seek peace within. I know that it's not easy in this new day and time for any of us. I don't know of a person on this earth who isn't faced with issues on a daily, but like the old man said to me just the other day, "Only the strong survive!"

I'm a Leo, so I'm not just going to survive, I'm going to thrive and reach for the stars. That statement he told me is nothing but the truth. You gotta have rhino skin to survive these tough times. Not everyone is going to have your back. You won't always have the support from the ones closest to you. So, I take my hats off to all of you who continue to grind hard for what you believe in. Nobody's perfect. Don't beat yourself up when you feel overwhelmed. We are diamonds made to shine in the darkest of times. Never let them see you sweat. At the end of this life, we all have a story to tell, and here's mine.

Sometimes life itself can throw you a curve ball, and you can either swing at the ball and hit it outta the park or let it go by and not swing at it at all. It's totally up to you. God gave us choices to make. The three most important choices you will ever make are who's your master, who's your mate, and what's your mission. Is money your master? Is your mate the right one for you? What are you here for? Those choices will dictate your future. When that curve ball comes at you—because trust me, it will—you need to be ready. And I'm not talking about a baseball. I'm talking about that moment in time when things are going right and then all of a sudden, BAM! You get some unexpected news. What's your next move? You can choose to be that hero and swing at life to make magic happen or you're gonna be a loser and give in to the struggle.

For me, I want to be great.

Here's the thing, though—because, you know, there's always a thing. With greatness sometimes comes sacrifice. But the ultimate goal is to never sacrifice your queen. And that may be one of the biggest mistakes I find myself making—sacrificing my queen and not giving her the time that she needed from me in our relationship. With that being said, I am going through a divorce. After twenty years of building a family with four kids, I have to go on and try to make it all make sense. It's hard because my two daughters, Kamryn and Chase, mean the world to me. Not to mention my two sons, who are great as well. It really hurts me to the core of my soul that I'm not with them every day when I wake up in the morning.

The best part for me about being a father is knowing that my kids love and respect me. However, even when I was at home, I was always gone because I was trying to make my mark in the world as a chef. I feel like a doctor, always on call. Between catering, co-owning In a Minute Cafe, and cooking for big-name celebrities and professional athletes daily at their mansions and yachts, I was pretty busy. Most in the culinary world would have considered me as being very successful!

Reginald O. Mack, also known as Chef RŌM, was becoming a household name in the the DMV area. It's to the point where when I now order food from Instacart for myself, the drivers who deliver the food to me are saying, "Hey aren't you Chef RŌM?" I'll tell them, "Yeah, that's me" with a slight chuckle. The problem is I lost sight of what it meant to be a good husband and even better father.

See, it's more than providing financially. Emotional support is just as important if not more, and that's where I missed the mark. I was so wrapped up in my own head and day-to-day hustle that I didn't take the time to plan dates just because or send flowers and candies randomly to show my wife that she mattered the most to me above all things. I can't lie. I took her for granted. What I thought I was doing was showing my wife and kids that a strong work ethic was the key to success. But now I ask myself, "What is success if the ones you love the most aren't there to share your triumphs with you?" I tried to instill in my kids as their father that they could be anything they wanted to be and that their dreams would be a reality if they woke up and worked hard for what they wanted in life. My thing was leading by example, and that meant I was always working to provide for the family. I figured that at the end of the day, as long as I paid the mortgage and put food on the table, that was sufficient. I'm learning the hard way that it's never enough. You have to constantly make your family a number-one priority at all times!

When Dr. Ashanti asked me to be a part of the Girl Dad Project, I didn't think that I was the right candidate for the assignment because I have two boys and two girls. She told me that it's fine because she believed that I still needed to share my story. When she asked me months ago, I wasn't going through what I'm going through now. As the time got near and the deadline approached, I really didn't know where to begin. I say that it must be divine intervention because writing this is actually helping me to cope with the pain. I'm being transparent about my life in hopes that what I'm going through helps the next man who may be going through something similar. I'm here now, and the only way that I could complete this assignment was to involve my two daughters in the writing process itself.

I recently asked my two girls, Kamryn and Chase, what I meant to them as a father, and they blew my mind with their responses! This is what my youngest fifteen-year-old princess, Chase, who has dreams of going to school in France for fashion design, had to say:

Growing up as my father's daughter, he was away from home a lot, and I was raised by my mother most of the time. But whenever we did spend time together, it was more special. My mom was always mad at something, and whenever she got mad at me, I just ignored it. But it was always scarier when father was mad. He was always the nice, loving parent. Even though he rarely ever got mad, when he did, he'd bring the thunder.

He would always encourage us to strive for our dreams and work hard for what we wanted. To me, he was one of my biggest inspirations. Seeing him work so hard every day trying to become a chef made me believe that one day I could do that too to accomplish my dreams. Even though after work he'd always complain, when it was all said and done, he never gave up because he had a family to support and a dream to achieve. Because of this, I didn't mind if he wasn't home much. Whenever he spoke to us, he'd tend to turn it into a lesson. He'd often speak in quotes and made me look at him as a wise person, someone I could learn from.

When she sent me that paragraph and I read it, I felt every word because it was so spot on and sincere. I mean like really, she absorbed so much from me from my actions. I had no idea she felt this way about me. At that point I knew that I wasn't a failure at being a father. My mark was made in her heart, and she knew my intentions were pure. I'm never giving up on my family! We may be miles apart, but our hearts will be close forever!

Kamryn, aka Queen K is a brilliant individual. She's the one who grew up hearing impaired and has cochlear implants. And at the age of twenty years old, she has never expressed that she has had any issues at doing anything. She spoke at her high school graduation and got a round of applause for her speech about never giving up. I was so happy and proud to be her father! This is what she said about me:

Father. Dad. Pops. Baba. Papi.

You can call it many things, but in the end, they'll always be the protector, the provider, and the disciplinarian. People say that it's easier for a father to have children than children to have a real father, and I wholeheartedly agree because my dad, Reginald O. Mack, is one of the realist people that I know on this planet called Earth. He is a natural-born leader, a true hustler, a man with a plan, but most of all, a man of God. There isn't a day that goes by where he doesn't slip some of his words of wisdom into my head, and I'm very grateful for that because it helped me become the person that I am to this day. I love the corny jokes he shares with me. I love the positive energy he brings my way, and I love the love that's in his heart. Nobody is perfect, yet he's the best dad to me. I promise I'll feel this way always and forever because there's nothing I would change.

Reading that really brought me to tears because I understood that my kids get me! They really feel me and know that I'm there for them even when I'm not around. But trust me, I'm grinding so hard now so that we can spend more time later. And if I die in the grind, I'll die trying and knowing that I made a positive impact on their lives! That's all I can do, right? That's all we can do as parents, period! We are given these seeds of life called kids, and our duty is to provide light (insight) and water (food) so that our greatest treasures can grow to be brilliant adults one day and they can in return grow their own families and nurture them with some of the values we instill in them. That's my focus.

In these days and times, it's really difficult for us all because of all the negativity that surrounds us on social media and TV. We all need to take a media diet from time to time to clear our heads of the garbage that we hear and see. If we as parents don't instill values in our kids early, they will easily be lead astray and fall victim to a false identity and will never reach their full potential as the true kings and queens they were destined to be. Listen, Satan's main purpose is to kill the seeds so that the God in them doesn't flourish. It's our mission as parents to not let that happen. This is why I'm always sending my kids positive videos and quotes so that I know they get a good dose of truth in their system and not a watered-down version of it.

Now while I'm adapting to my current living situation without my kids, it is really difficult for me. I always had both of my parents around, but my soon-to-be-ex-wife didn't. She had her mom around, and now the cycle repeats itself because our kids are with their mom. But what I want to do is set goals for myself in this new day that I'm facing with all the challenges I'm up against as a newly single parent. My first goal is to let my voice be heard. That's what I'm doing with this project. In order to be a better person and father, I have to accept my faults and begin to fix them one day at a time.

Hey look, I don't know who this is for, but I was once told that the hardest life will make the greatest impact. Boy is it hard going through a divorce after twenty years and going from having a whole family who loves you to having to live life fighting to keep that love alive. We built a lot of memories during that time. But now it's a new day, so we will have to build new memories. I'm not trying to make this a sad story, but it is. I'd be a liar if I told you that I didn't shed tears from looking at the pictures of my kids on the walls when I come home at night. I'm hurting but I'm also healing at God speed. I'm keeping my faith and keeping the scripture of Romans 8:28 near and dear to my heart: "All things work together for the good for those who love the Lord!" (KJV). That was my Uncle Odis's favorite scripture. God rest his soul. He also told me back when my wife and I were separated before that all we could do as men was work on bettering ourselves.

THE CHARGE

As a Girl Dad, I will make it a priority to spend more time with my daughters while I can. I think we all should focus on spending more time with our daughters because time is something we can't get back. And they grow up so fast. It feels like I'm missing a lot of key moments in their lives. Good thing we have FaceTime so I can check up on them from time to time while I'm out on the daily grind just so they know I'll always be dad. The funny thing is they didn't even call me by the name daddy. Instead, my name from them was cheffy!

DEAR DAUGHTER

Dear Daughter,

I'd like to take this opportunity to tell you that I'm your number-one fan. I love you with all my heart! If you ever need a helping hand or a shoulder to cry on, don't ever hesitate to call on me. While you grow up and mature into young women, I want you to remember that you are royalty and cut from the King's cloth. Don't let anyone tell you different. Know your value, and most importantly, know yourself. Be a leader and don't follow the crowd. Seek joy, not happiness, because happiness is an emotion that comes and goes. You want to be able to wake up with joy in your heart and a sound peace of mind. That can only be achieved with God as your foundation. Trust and believe in God for wisdom and guidance to get you through all things. I'm your earthly father, but you belong to God.

In conclusion, I say thank you, Father God, for allowing me to be a witness of Your amazing grace. You took me from selling narcotics to selling crab cakes. It was and will always be Your plan for my life. You've brought me so far, and I know You aren't done with me yet! I may be becoming a great chef, but God, please allow me to become a greater father.

Chapter 9
POWER IN THE PAUSE

by Kelly Burgess

I have ten kids.

Yep ten.

Three of them are girls.

The running joke in the family is that all the boys came because I was trying to have another girl; I love being a Girl Dad that much. But I have to be honest with you. I wish mine was a story of ten children; one wife; and a home full of happiness, joy, and love.

It's not.

It's still a great story, but it's also real life.

I have ten kids.

Three daughters.

One of whom is my biological daughter.

This is the story of my journey with her told through two shared memories—a diner and a cruise—and what those memories have taught me about being a Girl Dad.

Recently my daughter Lori and I had an interesting conversation.

"Babe, remember that writing project I was telling you about?" my text said. "I think I asked you about ten memories. I have a list of my own. Would love to share it."

"Yes," she replied. "I would love to talk through your list and vice versa! When would you like to do that?"

Interestingly, she wanted to *hear* the list, in real time, preferring not to see the list ahead of our phone call. Girls—they love the mystery of the reveal! So, we FaceTimed later that same evening and shared our lists.

One memory at a time.

Taking turns, like a game of memory tennis.

My list of ten was smorgasbord of recollections—the good, the bad, the happy and the intensely painful. The memories had names, like the chapter titles, each evoking strong images and feelings. There was my list:

- The "Darin" Letter
- The Cell Phone

- Five-Year-Old Birthday Party
- The Prom Dress
- The Cruise
- I Don't Want to Visit Anymore
- The Thirty-Mile Cry
- Marathon Softball Game
- Annie
- Momma Lo's Video
- The "Photos"
- The "Sean" Experience

Her list was equally varied with recollections of tremendous highs and crushing lows.

- The Bat, the Car, and the Dad Fart
- The Conductor
- Oodles of Noodles
- Sleep Walking and CPS
- Being Present – Feb 2020
- "Daddy" by Beyonce

- The Cruise
- The Diner
- The Assault Reveal
- Airport Birthday Surprise
- Rotten Potatoes

Twenty-three memories between us. Two memories that made both of our lists:

- The Diner
- The Cruise

I felt privileged to be in a position where my daughter would even share those memories with me because there was a time when she wouldn't have let me in that space.

Flash back five years to the most difficult time with my daughter Lori. "The Diner" is the name we share for a conversation that took place in the fall of 2016 at a diner in a College Park, MD, a small college town near where I grew up. There had been tension in our relationship since her mom and I had split up fifteen years earlier. Over the years, the bitterness over my leaving had welled up in Lori to a point where she really wasn't feeling me at all. We would have some good moments, but she made it clear that I wasn't in her inner circle. I was her father but not a dad. Things had gotten to a point where we needed to meet, so the diner was where we agreed to talk.

During our time, Lori revealed how my past actions had caused her so much pain. She sobbed uncontrollably in the middle of this diner. I could only sit there, owning this pain that I had caused. The hardest part was seeing years of pain erupt from my daughter, spill from her eyes, and not being able to do anything to undo the hurt. I was fully at fault, and I had to just sit there in it. Once she was able to finish speaking, I could only utter:

"I am so sorry that I caused you much pain."

That conversation shook me to my core. It opened a newfound insight for how my daughter processed my actions. When I left her mom and started another life, it irrevocably changed the trajectory of Lori's life. She felt the dual pull of wanting to love me and have me in her life *and* being fearful and repulsed by me because of the hurt I had caused. As painful as that conversation was, in hindsight, it was the catalyst for healing and a watershed moment in our relationship. It lanced the boil of poisoned emotions between us and started a process of healing where she felt heard by me and less hurt by me. That conversation humbled me and made me internalize in a more complete way how my abandonment had impacted her.

However, all things work out for good, because without the pain of "The Diner," there would be no privilege of "The

Cruise"—the second of the two memories that made both our lists. Lori and I joke that I was sloppy seconds as a choice of travel companion for the cruise. The cruise was meant to be a trip for her and Darin, her boyfriend, but by 2020, their relationship was on the rocks. But the cruise tickets had been purchased, so I was the fill-in. As Lori and I recollected that event, we remembered how we almost didn't make the trip—how we almost missed our plane to Florida and the ship once we got to Florida. We laughed about being the second to last people to board the ship in February 2020, just a month before the entire world shut down because of COVID. But we did make it, and the nine days we spent at sea were some of the best days of my life and hers too. It taught me the importance of time and experiences—that at the end of the day, you simply want to be able to spend time doing what you love to do with the people you love. The four years between "The Diner" and "The Cruise" were like a graduate degree in father-daughter relationships. Lori and I healed hurts and forged a new path. That's not to say that we haven't had our moments since 2020, but the deposits we made in our relationship gave us enough in the emotional bank account to stay positive.

"The Diner" and "The Cruise" remind me that as Girl Dads, we have tremendous power. You are the template, the mold, and the apex of what it means to be a man. If you have a harmonious relationship with her mom, if you are married or in a monogamous, committed relationship, then her mom will amplify and affirm your positive role in your daughter's life. Your daughter will subconsciously learn that men can be counted upon for protection, provision, and positive presence.

If you are not in the same house or if you are thinking about leaving, I need to be straight with you: your work is going to be harder, but you can do it. Some days, you will feel like you are fathering through a thick layer of smog and noise and that your best efforts to display that same love, protection, and presence as an in-home dad are muted and stifled. You might feel like it takes so much more effort to have an impact, to be counted, or to be seen. My challenge to you is to count the cost of not being in the house with your daughter if you are thinking of leaving your house. Think about:

How many bedtime stories are you willing to give up?

How many times of doing hair or movie nights snuggled on the couch would you like to give away?

How many first dates do you want to forfeit?

How many cries on the shoulder do you want to relinquish?

How many games do you want someone else to pick her up from?

How many times will you get to walk her down the aisle or dance with her at her wedding?

As a Girl Dad, get good at bandaging emotional wounds. Sometimes the best application of medicine is "I'm sorry, I blew it. Please forgive me."

I'm sorry.

I blew it.

Please forgive me.

Those three simple statements change the power dynamic in your relationship with your daughter. In those statements, she will see you as humble and human. She will let her guard down and allow you the emotional space to walk your way back to her. Whether you are thousands of miles away from your daughter or with bar, plexiglass and barbed wire between you, those words transcend time and space. They destroy barriers and dig up the fallow ground so that the seeds of healing and forgiveness can take root. Get good at saying "I am sorry."

As a Girl Dad, you will need to pursue your daughter relentlessly, especially when she seeks to naturally break away from you during her "mean-ager" years. Sometimes, pursuit is a morning "I am thinking about you." text. Sometimes, it's an invitation to coffee or lunch or dinner. Sometimes it is a request for advice because you value her insights and intuition as a woman and her unbiased perspective. Pursue her consistently with flowers, her favorite gift, or a surprise visit. Pursue, pursue, pursue. By doing this, you subconsciously let her know that she is worthy of being chased, that the mountain should be scaled for her, and that she doesn't need to settle.

As a Girl Dad, you will have the opportunity to make and break promises. Keep your promises, and you'll be cemented in her life as the standard for her future life partner. Break promises, and you will create the model from which she will run, vowing to never have a man with those qualities. Master being the kind of man who does what he says he will do, when he says he will do it, whether he feels like it or not. By keeping your promises, your daughter will seek and find men who are dependable, trustworthy, and consistent. Promises are powerful reminders that you have prioritized her in your life and that she can count on you when the chips are down.

A WORD TO DISTANT GIRL DADS

To the Girl Dads who are not in their daughters' daily lives. Maybe you've sat with the phone in your hand about to call or text your daughter and then told yourself, "Nah. She don't want to talk to me right now. She's busy, maybe doing something with her friends. She's good."

Sometimes, we make ourselves ghosts, apparitions, or shadows of an authority figure. We try to father from the wings, staying backstage because of shame. Please don't let shame and regret push you to the edges in your daughter's life. Get to a point where you can own whatever you have done to drive a wedge between your daughter and you. Get on the other side of the net with her and have the problems between you two end on the other side of the net.

Maybe your last conversation with your daughter was the worst conversation you've ever had with her. Maybe she said some things to you that were so painful that you felt you needed to distance yourself from her. Maybe she told you that she needed some distance from you, that you weren't allowed into certain realms of her life, because you stepped out of the priority position in her life. You chased other things or other people, but during your chasing, your daughter was not standing still waiting for you to come back to yourself, frozen in time as if you could just press pause on her life and she would be there—the same little girl who once saw you as a hero. While you were chasing, she was evolving and morphing into a woman who was left to fill in the blanks about her worth, fill in the gaps in your biography, and generally keep life moving. She kept it moving until the day you realized that you have missed entire swaths of her life and she is not the little girl anymore, but rather a powerful woman who can expertly articulate the hurt you've caused, blow by painful blow. The best thing you can do for at that point is…

Sit there and listen.

Just listen.

Fully, with your ears *and* your eyes and your body posture and the little "uh-huh"s and head nods that let her know that you are completely dialed in.

Listen to both her explicit words and her implicit messages.

Because if she is talking to you, she is building a bridge to you.

If you have caused her pain, you must own all of it. You may have to own it on several, separate occasions because life events will trigger memories in her, and those triggers can make the hurt as fresh as the day it first happened. Men feel pain. Women feel pain in 3D. They feel pain for the community. It's as if they take pain and it resonates within them and interacts with the pain and empathy of others, and that whole pain-empathy cycle reverberates into a chorus of pain and empathy. Our daughters feel deeply and in cycles, and it can seem that the pain is never resolved. I've learned that this is simply how women process hurt, and the revisiting of it through conversation is their way of affirming that their instincts were correct and that the 360-degree view of their pain was not an aberration.

THE CHARGE

As a Girl Dad, you will have losses, especially if you are not in the house with your daughter. You will be compared to other men; you may have to even work through and around the authority of another man in your daughter's life. That is a tough pill to swallow, but swallow it and then continue to pursue your daughter and a relationship with her as fully as circumstances allow. If you are not in a committed, monogamous relationship with her mom, do all you can to make your co-parenting relationship, peaceful, healthy, and effective. Never speak negatively about her mom; silence is easier to walk back from than vitriol.

As a Girl Dad, you have many roles—provider, protector, and preparer, to name a few. Wherever you are in your journey with your daughter, you can do small things today to let her know she is valued, that she is seen, and that you are there for her. Whether you are near or far, whether she is a little girl, a teenager, a young woman, or an adult with children and a spouse, you are a vital part of her life, and she wants to hear from you. As long as you are reading this, you have time to make amends, affirm her, and have a positive impact in her life. God Bless and Happy Fathering.

DEAR DAUGHTER

A word to daughters reading this, young or old, and especially if you have had to navigate life without your father in your life on a day-to-day basis.

I see you.

I see your power, your value, and your resilience

I see your immense intelligence, your fears, and your wonderings.

They are all valid. You are not crazy.

I see the nights you have fallen asleep sobbing, wondering if you are good enough, if you are a priority, if you count.

I see your attempts to mute the pain through myriad medications of alcohol; drugs; work; and toxic, unbalanced relationships; struggling to break the allure of those things.

I see you yearning to see your parents reconcile, year after year, subconsciously hoping against hope that they will get back together and that you can be a family again. I see you grieving as you lay that same desire in a grave, the corpse of a prior life that will not be resurrected. I see you do the mental calculus, sigh and say, "Oh well," and numb yourself from feeling the pain of the permanence of the change in your family. It's a transformative moment for you, a thrusting into adulthood and the knowledge that there will be things that you simply cannot change and that a life you once knew will not be the same again. That is one of the most difficult things to experience, and I see that and sit with you in that space.

I see you trusting yourself again to love and being open to a better tomorrow.

I see you building confidence in yourself and your decision making. In your ability to not settle just because your feel the gnaw of loneliness.

I see you whole, healed, and helping other girls and women to walk the path that you have walked. It is because you have experienced such acute pain *and* processed it in a thorough and healthy way that you are uniquely equipped to assist another on their journey.

I see you forgiving your father and maybe eventually calling him dad or daddy again, maybe even for the first time.

I see you introducing him to his grandchildren and your life partner.

I see you sitting by yourself, but not alone, maybe in your favorite room in your house of your favorite third place, taking a deep breath, sighing, and realizing that you have come so far in your journey.

I see you.

My prayer is that you find safe spaces to unpack those memories and hopes that you can bring your whole self to the life you have to live.

My prayer is that you are not hindered by bitterness, unforgiveness, and unrealistic expectations of yourselves. Some burdens are too great to carry alone. They are meant to be divided and shared with another.

I pray that you find a counselor who can lighten that load and help you carry those burdens, sort them out, and put them to rest at the proper time and in the proper way.

Chapter 10

PRESENCE OVER PRESENTS

by Thomas G. Warner, Jr.

I am a humble native of Atlanta, Georgia who has always had a burning passion inside of me in all things that I have been a part of. My parents were never married, and I grew up as the youngest and only son of three children without my dad in the house, although we stayed in constant contact. Growing up in Perry Homes, one of the roughest neighborhoods in Atlanta, I have always pushed to find a way out as I transitioned from elementary school to middle school having to witness gang violence amongst my peers in the city of Atlanta. This was during a time where gangs like "Bloods" and "Crips" and were materializing.

During my younger years, I was heavy into visual arts until the summer of my freshman year of high school. I was asked to play trumpet in the Archer High School Band, where my sisters and cousins were all members. The band director at the time was Nathan Grigsby, also a trumpet player, but also an outstanding pianist and vocalist. Because my cousins played percussion instruments, I was determined to follow in their footsteps. Unbeknownst to me, Mr. Grigsby needed trumpet players. The summer leading to high school was my first time picking up the trumpet and learning to play it in a week. After consistent playing and getting on all my neighbors' nerves, I quickly moved to the rank of section leader by the first football game. Since that moment, music became my way out, and I never looked back.

Over the course of my years in high school, I was recruited to be a church musician by a great group of trumpet players at Mt. Carmel Baptist Church in Atlanta, where my band director, Nathan Grigsby, was the minister of music. Those trumpet players, Bobbiedee, Erroyl, and Robert, became my brothers, and of course, Nathan was a mentor for life. From here, and eventually playing at other churches with this same core group of musicians, my passion for music grew deeper. This led me to pursue a bachelor's, master's, and doctor of philosophy in music education and eventually to North Carolina A&T State University as an assistant band director and music professor.

There were many musical and life lessons to be learned amongst these men of music. They laughed and cried together. They saw ups and downs together; they celebrated education; and they even saw relationships grow together, stay together, and grow apart. As I matriculated through college and my professional life, I always had an insatiable passion and loyalty to those around me, including these gentlemen I consider my family. Most importantly, these opportunities of growth showed me how to be a father and husband and to always have faith in God.

In September of 2010, the fatherhood journey for Thomas Gregory Warner, Jr. started with one of the greatest additions to my life with Thomas Richard Allen Warner (TRA), the big brother. Although it can be stated on many levels how wonderful of a big brother Thomas is, let's fast forward five years.

Those who are familiar with the band world or considered "band heads," are familiar with the Honda Battle of The Bands. It happened annually in Atlanta at the Georgia Dome, now Mercedes-Benz Stadium. The night before Reece came into the world, band practice was one of those things that you really wanted to end sooner than later. In addition, the directors and staff were still cleaning a field show to be ready in a few days. Eventually it became later, but more specifically around eleven at night. Just as I began to finally drift off to sleep, I received a call from my wife around three in the morning saying the pains wouldn't stop and that she was heading to the hospital. So, with absolutely no sleep, I jumped in the car for a hard fought five-and-a-half-hour drive from Greensboro, North Carolina to Atlanta, Georiga to arrive around eight in the morning.

After what seemed to be maybe thirty minutes to an hour in January of 2015, Reece Madison Warner, Daddy's Sugar Plum Reece Cup, was gifted to this world. I could not let her out of my sight, even when they took her away to be foot printed and do all the special things that nurses do. As the day passed and everything was in order, Reece was transported home. After a few days, I had to travel back to North Carolina to gather my band director uniform and other things and drive back to Atlanta, because who's thinking about band while this beautiful princess was waiting on me? Seeing as this was only the second semester of my first year working at North Carolina A&T, this was the first real struggle as a dad.

With the family still having domicile in Atlanta, I wanted to be sure that I was at all events, birthday parties, and firsts. This meant driving and burning gas, sometimes every weekend or every couple of weeks. My only thought process was always being there no matter the cost or the toll it put on me. Being a band director on the collegiate level made me realize that there are people who care about you and there are people who couldn't care less, and this same subjective thought transferred to life outside of band, music, and higher education.

As Reece grew and developed into the blossoming little sugar plum she is today, I had begun questioning everything, which also included decisions for the big brother and their mom. What was my future going to look like in my current employment situation? Was my family ever going to move to be in the same place where I worked? Would there be pay raises in the future? How was I going to balance work and personal life with this new life I must protect? Did anyone even care?

One of the biggest turning points of my life was when I was diagnosed with some weird form of a respiratory infection. Being loyal to my job and my students, I didn't want to seem weak or incompetent by not being there. With all the pain I was enduring at rehearsals and at an away game, I had to retreat to my studio apartment for about a week. This was during preparation for the greatest homecoming on Earth. No one knew where I was, and hardly anyone checked on me. The symptoms were all too familiar now but unknown at the time. I still believe it was some early form of COVID-19. I also believe God kept me alive because of my passion and drive to complete my God-given tasks that were set before me.

After a trip to my personal physician and about seventy pounds lighter, I slowly regained my strength. However, the thought process was different. I could not be the strong father and husband that I was perceived to be. I was weak and vulnerable physically and mentally. From here, work-life balance became a priority. I ate healthier, went to the gym more, and got more sleep, which was something that I struggled with, just because I wanted to make sure I was doing my part in all areas of my life. I thought about being able to see my children more and being able to watch them grow up and experience the important things in their lives.

It was always important for me to be there as a dad for Thomas as well. To teach him to be a man and great person in society. For Reece, I wanted to be sure I was always there to give her a thousand kisses and show her what the true unconditional love of a man for a woman feels like, all while taking her to get her favorite toy, watching her play and laugh with her brother, and making her favorite Daddy-style pancakes and breakfast menu items. Realistically, I didn't have a close bond with my parents, but I had great positive influences and persons who showed me great examples, and there were several pivotal life lessons that I saw in those young musicians I played with at church in high school on through college and into my career. Some of them had daughters, and they always had positive relationships with them. They were excellent examples, but I wanted more for my relationship with Reece.

Another pivotal moment in my life was struggles with the housing market. As I worked out of state, I thought about the decision to rent or buy a house. Rent was the best option with the uncertainty. This was pivotal because I had to make decisions regarding living situations for my family that were out of control. The landlord at the time decided that they were putting the house up for sale, but I had no desire to purchase. The landlord gave me thirty days to move. Although there were two young ones in the house, I especially did not want little Reece Cup to experience unnecessary relocations at such a young age. This included taking off time from work to drive down from North Carolina and move an entire house with the help with only a few fraternity brothers in a matter of one day. This was a mental and physical strain on me, but eventually it all worked out so that the family could have a comfortable roof over their heads. In the end, it sparked another fire in me to ensure that my children did not know the details of the situation and didn't have to worry about anything happening to them.

A most recent pivotal moment was family ties. Over the years, I have had to had to deal with some life-changing situations regarding family—some that made strong and some that broke me down. No matter the situation, I kept faith in God and always soared as a leader and an example. I am a family-oriented person who will always put my family first. This has not been the best of times in recent years with my family. I have tried on numerous occasions to have my children around my family, but recent differences and unwarranted actions caused me to pull away due to negativity. This made me consider how important it is to me that my children always have those positive environments. With Reece being the youngest, I didn't want her to have to experience these dysfunctional family elements, although TRA is mature enough to navigate through them. To the average person, it may be minor, but at this point in my life, I am all about positive and nurturing environments.

At this point, I have been working at North Carolina A&T for eight years. It breaks my heart every time I must be away from my kids, but Reece always shows the most emotion and displeasure when Daddy must go back to work. I believe that the bond with my daughter is pivotal in her personal growth, but my biggest fear is that she will get used to me always being at work. That is why work-life balance is so important to me. As a music professor on the higher education level, the duties and responsibilities are in addition to being a band director, which never stops when you are actively involved and part of one of the best bands and largest historically Black colleges and universities in the country. I could easily teach more than the normal load for a regular professor, which could max out all the seats in my class. It really can be taxing at times.

I absolutely love what I do in the music education profession, but I also want to make sure that if I cannot be home right now for the time being that I can frequently bond with my daughter. As I pursued my PhD, I was told to learn how to say no. This journey has taught me how to say no to a lot of things and a lot of people, not in a malicious way but more in a positive selfish way. It taught me how to put myself and my mental and physical health first. I must be strong for my sugar plum, Reece, and of course for her big brother, Thomas, whom she loves so dearly even when things are tough. In the end, the relationships are positive with positive outcomes, and they get to have Daddy more often.

During these trying times as a father traveling to earn and make master wages and to be more gainfully employed, I have had to reach out to a close circle of people who have my best interest at heart. A special group I reach out to is my "Hospitality Bruhs"—Paul, Rufus, Mo, and Sean—who share a special bond as Masons and Shriners. In addition are friends and colleagues Kevin and Will, who were in graduate school with me at Florida State University and are now part of a circle that can relate to the PhD process and family life. The most consistent resource has been my college band director and mentor, Mr. Eddie Ellis. He is probably the one person who can directly relate to my situation as a father in the band director roll. My relationship with Mr. Ellis began when I was a student at Morris Brown College, where I held leadership roles as trumpet section leader and as a drum major. It was your typical student-teacher relationship. My relationship grew when I became an assistant band director under Mr. Ellis at South Carolina State University.

As the years went on, my career took off, and I give credit to Mr. Ellis for the recommendations and opportunities post undergraduate. When I was a young, energetic music educator, I progressed through my profession and was elected and served as president of a national president for a music organization for HBCU band directors. Of course, these leadership roles add to the hustle and bustle of the already strenuous day-to-day life of the band director and music professor. I turned to Mr. Ellis, who has a daughter close to my age and who at the time had just given birth to her child. Many of the conversations between me and Mr. Ellis went from band to life situations, even down to Mr. Ellis saying how much he wanted to spend time with his grandson. This put a lot of things in perspective from my standpoint of being a Girl Dad.

With the success that Mr. Ellis has had, he has always circled back to his family. The bonding time with his children was important. This was a complete eye opener. As I continue my career path and all that God has in store for me, I look back and consider many colleagues who have passed away in their offices and on the job. I ask myself self, "Do I want to sacrifice time with my daughter or my family for a job that will replace me when I die?" With that in mind, I started taking things off my plate and taking more time off. There is still room for improvement, but it became necessary.

THE CHARGE

As a Girl Dad, I will prioritize time with my family while balancing a growing career. As a Girl Dad, I will balance work and life. Children are so precious, but the daughters usually have a stronger grip on the dads, so it hits differently when she smiles at, hugs, and kisses Daddy. I will listen to her heart and listen to her feelings. I want to be available for all that she does with no reservation so that she knows, without a doubt, that I love and care for her. This is key for my daughter's positive personal growth and will eventually help her in all areas of her life.

DEAR DAUGHTER

My prayer to my daughter is to always be genuine. Understand that fathers, especially Black fathers, have the weight of the world on them. We fight unseen battles all while trying to protect and provide for our families. I pray that God shapes your mind and heart to be one of understanding. I pray that He gives you the intelligence and zeal to make and reach your goals. I pray that He helps you to be strong and diligent in all your endeavors yet remain humble in all your movements. I pray that He allows you to find a husband who will support you and whom you will support with a clear and open heart to love and be a true example of love in a healthy and happy family environment.

Chapter 11

PRODIGAL GIRL DADS PROSPER

by Dr. Charles Lucious Perry

The book *Committed: Finding Love and Loyalty Through the Seven Archetypes* (Harra and Harra 2021) suggests various archetypes of people who fall in love. I found that I related to the character of the Hopeless Romantic, who best mates with Wounded Warriors. I have been searching for real love (Mary J. Blige is playing in my head) since I was that mannish little boy who snuck under the dining room table at the age of four to love at the hairy legs of the women my mother invited over for formal Sunday dinner. I've always admired women. That admiration has driven me to make very risky decisions in my life—multiple marriages, multiple households, and multiple offspring and life outcomes.

Some people prayed for me—my grandmother and mother. They were Baptist. However, there's a slight chance that my grandfather and father prayed as well. They were Methodist. Those prayers saved me from a life of perpetually swine-like behavior and certain doom and demise.

This story is about a prodigal, noncustodial father of three daughters, each from a different mother whom I loved and lost for various reasons. November Nicole (November) is the oldest, born in January 1972. Emerald (also known as Ebony), born February 9, 1977, was a love child of the mid-1970s, post-Civil Rights, Equal Educational Opportunities Act (EEOA), Environmental Protection Act (EPA), and riots. Yankee was born June 24, 1980, during a time when I was at the peak of my lunacy. The perpetual prayers of my parents and grandparents from days of old and from heaven were still overlooking me as I journeyed from lunacy to prodigality to becoming a father who cares immensely about embracing the future to create positive memories and seeding a legacy of sharing and giving to the future generations yet born.

NOVEMBER (JANUARY 28, 1972; LAKE CITY, FLORIDA)

November is my first born. I was a seventeen-year-old teenage parent and in a whirlwind of small-town fantasies of having a child with a seventeen-year-old girl (Vanity) on whom I had a crush since fifth grade. I was excited when November was born on January 28, 1972.

My family was in disbelief, particularly my daddy. Some attribute my daddy's subsequent illness to the fact he detested my teenage father status so much that he started to drink more and eventually suffered a paralyzing stroke. I remember carrying November when she was maybe two or three months old to see him, and he threw a fit, so much so that there was a public outburst of emotions between my daddy and me on that spring Saturday afternoon. Here's the odd thing—I became a girl daddy at seventeen. Vietnam was in full force and drafting young men at an accelerated rate. While the family dynamics were unfolding, I had taken the Armed Services Vocational Aptitude Battery (ASVAB) at school and convinced my father to help me sign up for the Air Force. Daddy hurriedly signed the necessary parental forms form me to enlist in the military at seventeen years old. Odd, isn't it, that I needed parental approval to join the military but not to become a parent?

I was with November for five months before departing for boot camp. In those five months I was enamored by the very thought of November and did not care what my friends were saying. I even took Vanity to the senior prom as parents.

When I left Lake City, Florida in 1972, my mother, Lue Berdia, and grandmother, Hannah, stepped up to the plate and became parents in my place. In effect, I was parenting through my mother and grandmother. From June 1972 to January 1973, my parenting was by letter.

From 1975 to 1980, I would see November only briefly when I would come home on leave. November spent a lot of time with my mother and grandmother. My grandfather had a liking for her as well. My mother would dress her up in ruffled dressed like Shirly Temple. Then, in 1980, Vanity moved to Seattle, Washington with all her daughters. From 1980 to 1990, I would have brief conversations with Vanity about November. But that was all.

In 1990, and I believe it to be true, November made a move in an attempt to be close to me. She applied for and got accepted to Virginia State University. She claimed she wanted to get out of the cold and be around more people who looked like she looked—Black. Well, I attempted to be a dad and travel to Petersburg, Virginia to see November and spend time with her. I would pick November up and bring her to spend the weekend with me in Upper Marlboro, Maryland. We would go to Metropolitan Baptist Church. I would stick my chest out and pronounce, "This is my oldest daughter, November." Well, money was tight on my end, and I could not help November with her college expenses. She left Virginia State during her freshman year. Our recently started relationship became further strained.

By 1995, November had gone back home and gotten a job. She entered University of Washington and was graduating in May 1995. I attended November's graduation. That was a wonderful moment. We took pictures, and I still display those pictures prominently in my living room. I was working on a federal contractor's job that caused me to travel to various cities in the United States. I would negotiate to secure assignments in Seattle so I would get a chance to see November. I would see her and spend a night with her. We grew slightly together in that manner. That's how we communicated for years.

In 2003, November wanted to move out of Seattle. She looked at several cities, including the DC Metro area. During her visit to the DMV in November 2003, I was hopeful that November would choose to be close to me, but we got into an argument that again strained our relationship. She abruptly left my house to stay with a friend for the rest of her stay in the DMV. Ultimately, November decided to move to the Dallas, Texas area in 2004. November made the choice to move to Texas and be near a childhood friend and the friend's family who—for the most part—had all moved from Seattle for some of the same reasons November wanted to move there: culture and weather. In any event, November's friends became her support system to help acculturate her to the Texas way of life.

From 2004 to 2011, November and I would talk over the phone periodically, get mad, then throw hints of wanting to get back together as father and daughter only to experience something else that would trip-wire our relationship into a strained posture and interaction. Months would go by without verbally speaking. Birthdays and holidays became pathways to at least send a card, text, or some messaging to communicate that we were still thinking of each other. November, using the internet as a medium, connected with a charming young man who eventually would become father of my granddaughter Alexis in 2011.

Since 2011, November and I continue the dance of a distant mother-father love-hate affair. Our last argument in 2021 brought back fifty years of uncertainty. As I look back on the fifty years that November and I have known each other, it has been non-custodial affair that has spilled over into a dysfunctional father-daughter relationship, camouflaging the hurt by expressions of love during birthdays and holidays.

EMERALD (BORN FEBRUARY 9, 1977; ROBINS AIR FORCE BASE, GEORGIA)

I arrived in the Republic of Korea on February 4, 1974, after being stationed at Malmstrom Air Force Base, Montana. I was nineteen years old and would become twenty while overseas. Vietnam was declared over, but Saigon had not fallen. Attending University of Maryland University College (now University of Maryland Global Campus) was a choice to keep my mind from going too far off the path of keeping up with my high school friends who opted to go straight to college in the face of Vietnam; they knew the student loan and Pell Grant process better than I did. I was starving for connecting with my culture I had left in Florida two years earlier. When I received my transfer orders announcing I was heading to Robins AFB, Georgia, I was excited to be back in the South and only two hundred miles away from my hometown, Lake City, Florida.

As soon as I could get settled at my new location, I visited the local education office because I wanted to continue what I started in Korea by attending college. I enrolled in Macon Junior College. I worked a job at Robins AFB that required me to work rotating shifts. I strategized to take classes that were taught day and night by the same professor to accommodate my rotating work schedule. I really enjoyed campus life. During one of my day-time classes, I noticed this big-legged, Afro-wearing, smooth-pecan-skinned woman. The woman's name was Yummy. The relationship continued, and we got married on January 6, 1976, and purchased a house that very same year. By May 1976, Yummy was pregnant with Emerald. I was an E4 in the US Air Force, and medical care was readily available; Emerald was born at Robins AFB on February 9, 1977—a year and one month from the time Yummy and I were married.

I knew Emerald as a baby—only as a baby.

I never denied Emerald. I knew her from the time I watched her come out of her mother's body in the delivery room—her extra fingers at birth, her health challenges with her eyes—but I did deny her of my direct and physical presence and expressive love when she was growing up. Further, I did deny her in that I did not pick her up every other week as the divorce decree had allowed. I was mad over the child support payment of $140 per month. Who knows what damage those denials have caused Emerald to this day? The ghostly answers push me toward a solution in visioning and legacy building to provide a therapy or salve for the wounds created by my absence and denials. Sometime in 1986 and before I moved from the Macon, Georgia area, Emerald came up to me after church one day in the parking lot (with her hand out), and I did not know how to respond. That was a deadening day. I did not see Emerald again until September 2004. Ironically, my son (her brother) moved back to Macon from Washington, DC, to attend college at my alma mater, Mercer University, in 2001. My son sought his sister out and built the bridge for me to cross over to build a relationship with Emerald. In all actuality, my life with her really began in 2004. Emerald was twenty-seven years old.

Since that time, Emerald (and her family) and I have exchanged gifts and visits during some holidays and seasonal events such as high school graduation and Army boot camp (for my oldest granddaughter). I use text to say hello, and this is an area that needs improving. Calls are seldom. It's not that I am shy, but phone conversations are not my norm. Perhaps standardizing a Zoom call would be fitting since Emerald lives in Macon, Georgia, and I live in Fort Washington, Maryland.

YIELDING (BORN JUNE 24, 1980; MACON, GEORGIA)

While transporting Emerald to day care, I met this young lady named Precious in April 1978. At the time I had transferred from Macon Junior College to Mercer University. I really loved Mercer University. I could say to my friends in Lake City, Florida, that I was in college and close to graduation.

Precious became pregnant in September 1979 with Yielding. Boy, did I cherish that moment. Yielding was born in Coliseum Hospital in Macon, Georgia. I wiped and cleaned Yielding as a baby and a toddler. She was born in the same zodiac time frame as Grandma Hannah (June 28) and me (July 9), so of course I told myself that we were super connected.

For six years, I built a relationship with Yielding by transporting her to Big Mama's and eventually Christian Day Care. I could tell Yielding was going to be a leader because of how she would interact with other kids.

We moved from Macon, Georgia, where I had lived for eleven years during which time three of my children were born, in 1986. We moved to Bolling AFB, District of Columbia. My relationship with Yielding was as a custodial father for her first ten years of life. I enjoyed the cuddling that living under one roof facilitates. To this day, I believe that the power of living under the same roof and being a custodial parent surpasses non-custodial [perceived] freedoms any day. And even after my misdeeds and inappropriate sexual behavior with other women, I foolishly disrupted my home and custodial parenting.

For most of Yielding's life, I have been in close proximity to her. From 1990 to 1998, my role became "taxi in chief" to get Yielding and her brother to and from special events at school, taking them to the doctor, and of course, paying child support. My relationship with Yielding was and is much different than my relationships with November and Emerald in that we lived with or near each other for eighteen years. Yielding saw my philandering and promiscuity—to my dismay, as many of the women with whom I cheated with were church women (the wounded warrior type). As a part of my custodial weekends, I would include the "woman for the season" in the dinner plans. Some of the women became jealous of my relationships with my younger two children. Looking back, while I was intelligent book wise, I was stupid man wise.

But my past—my mannish ways—would continue to haunt me. I left one relationship for another. Relationships tended to compete with Yielding for my time and attention (and her brother), and that competition would always result in strained relationships with my children—particularly my baby daughter.

My commitment to Yielding was different as well. I was ecstatic that Yielding was the valedictorian for her senior high school class. I was further excited that she wanted to go to a HBCU. I invested a lot of money into her education (though I learned later she opened credit cards to pay balances I didn't or couldn't make). So, I was super surprised that before she graduated, she announced she was in love with a guy. I protested. Insulated from my pleas, Yielding got married (I cried like a baby the day that she did) and has since birthed two daughters of her own (circa 2009 and 2015, respectively). The birth of those girls has definitely been a lifeline of new experiences and explorations. Yielding often speaks of creating positive memories for her daughters. I think Yielding is also expressing the sentiment of November and Emerald as well.

One of the most comfortable things I enjoy with Yielding is living in the same geographical area, even though that does not guarantee frequent visiting and outings. I use texting to keep communications fluid. I may have to advance to Zoom and TikTok to enhance daughter-dad communications.

The daughter-dad relationship that I enjoy with all of my daughters (though they are from different mothers; and that does matter) is best characterized by hope, vision, and legacy. My past is not prologue to my future (Shakespeare, *The Tempest*, 1611). A pessimistic view of my non-custodial, prodigal philandering, and promiscuity would suggest that I am doomed and that my children would reject me. However, the prevailing prayers of my ancestors continue to inspire me to do the right thing concerning my children. Whether it is the Baptist or Methodist underpinnings of my ancestors that guided their love for me and my upbringing, I am glad they prayed for me (for they did not spare the rod and spoil the child). Moreover, I am glad God is a merciful God who was and is very much in tune with His mission for my life. Thus, my vision and mission to November, Emerald, and Yielding is to change the narrative of my past and to continuously improve upon envisioning a future Girl Dad life that is driven by visions and legacies, full of possibilities in every imaginable aspect of life.

In a practical sense, acknowledging but not swimming in the past, embracing the future, and valuing legacies are the cornerstones of our future daughter-dad relationships. New life awaits me and my daughters because of the reflections in this chapter.

THE CHARGE

As a Girl Dad, I will have big dreams regarding all of my children and grandchildren. It is through their experiences that I see my future. As a Girl Dad, I will look forward to the visions and legacies we will create and experience together.

DEAR DAUGHTER

Dear Daughter,

My letter to you is based on my embrace and love of biblical passages that guide our way. My letter speaks to our future and to our legacy. I opted not to dwell on the past. Instead, I would like to share with you what is currently in my heart. My life has been enriched because of your birth. In fact, your birth helped me to go through my "prodigal father" years of philandering and promiscuity with shame; and that shame proved to be sobering as I reflected on my responsibility to you as a father. You know the story of the prodigal son who wanted to live largely and take his inheritance before it was time (Luke 15). His father honored his request, and the prodigal son plundered all of his resources that he eventually had to eat with the swine. Well, my dear, I did eat with the swine, and it was in that state that I called to God to deliver me from myself. God is a merciful God. Hence, my pursuit now as a father is to encourage you from two points of view. Habakkuk 2 and Proverbs 13:22 are two key messages that I share with you, and I continue to grow and live out your experiences as daughter and dad. Daughter, please know that I am excited about our future as we envision the change we seek in the recreational, familial, religious, educational, social, travel, and financial areas of our lives. I am encouraged to live on and to make it a high priority to communicate better using the latest technology to exchange our dreams and aspirations. Here's to love, here's to life, and here's to you.

REFERENCES

Harra, C. & Harra, A. (2021). *Committed: Finding Love and Loyalty Through the Seven.*

Archetypes. Newman Springs Publishing. ISBN 978-1-63692-756-5-51695.

Masters & Masters. (1972, 2008). *The Joy of Sex: The Timeless Guide to Lovemaking.* Harmony Publishers. ISBN 978-0-307-58778-7.

Shakespeare, W. (1611). *The Tempest* in William Frye (1959 ed.). Pelican. Pp 1 – 10.

ISBN 978-0-14-071415-9.

Chapter 12
PAY ATTENTION

by Ashanti Bryant Foster

DADDY'S GIRL DIALOGUES

Being a daddy's girl isn't as easy as it looks. Yes, I know it looks glamorous with all of the love and attention we get from our fathers, but it's quite consuming when you consider other people in your life. When you think about daddy's girl, you think about us being wrapped around their fingers and them giving us anything and everything we want. But that's not the entire story. As growing and grown women, we have a very high standard when dealing with other men in our lives, and, albeit unconsciously, we look for our father's traits in our mates. We expect nothing less than what daddy would do. We aren't easily impressed, we know all the guy codes, and we know how to wait patiently for doors to be opened. Now that doesn't mean we can't open our own doors. In fact, daddy's girls, although they may call on daddy to do lots of things for them, learn from daddy how to do it for themselves. We are independent and don't rely on others to get the job done. No is not our favorite word because daddy doesn't say it often, but when he does, we respect it because we know he only wants the best for us.

Our moms don't get how daddies could be the apple of our eyes when they do all the work. But they don't do all the work; daddies teach us the hidden curriculum of life, and that is not easy. Daddies have to balance letting us fall down in order to get tough with catching us in midair so that we feel no pain. Single moms, especially, feel like they do everything under the sun and moon for the child, yet we girls always find a way to hold our fathers in high regard. We cherish every item and activity that comes from our daddies. We protect him and take up for him. No one can love me like my daddy can. I know sometimes moms don't get it. And as much as we try to help them understand that daddies never do anything wrong in our eyes, they want us to see the husband's flaws. The problem is that our lens as daughters will never shift to any other lens. We can't see him as the imperfect husband who doesn't get everything right, but we can see him as the daddy that lives life in front of us so that we learn the good and the bad. My daddy wasn't even active in the church until I was a mother of my own six children, but he prayed over us, led grace for dinner, and provided sound advice in decision making. He taught us right from wrong and instilled values of responsibility, integrity, and cooperation in us. God was in him all along. Even though he stayed home when we went to church, I believe that God spoke to and through our head of the household and gave him the wisdom to ensure that our family thrived. My daddy has taught me so much over the years, and I am proud to be his daughter.

ONE MOUTH, TWO EARS

Growing up as the only child in the house for five years equated to me being in the company of mainly adults all the time. From socials held at my home to learning the "being in grown folks' business" lesson the hard way, I learned how to go back and forth in discussion and became a great debater. Even today, I still like to argue. For me it's the intellectual sparring and not the negative connotation that arguing poses. I'm like my daddy in that respect. He loves to have friendly debates, get the last word, and be right in friendly banter.

I will always remember what daddy would say when my spirit of interrupting people as they were making their points occurred. He'd ask me, "You know why God gave you two ears and one mouth, right?" I would get so annoyed when he said that, partly because he was right. Of course, I answered with my rehearsed response, "So I could listen twice as much as I speak." I understood that God had blessed me with the ability to listen, but, in the end, my goal was to get my point across and get other people to think how I thought. I didn't realize then, as a teenager, that understanding other people's perspectives as well as having empathy and understanding were what

I should be seeking. It was more important for me to be right, even when I realized I was wrong during the debate. I held strong to my point and deflected to another point to stay in the fight. I witnessed my father in many conversations with my mom when I knew he was right, but instead of trying to prove his point and make her see it like he saw it, he would listen.

Now Daddy is a human calculator—a mathematical genius! The man can stand in a room and tell you the dimensions and how many cans of paint you need to get the job done. Don't get me started on multiplying recipes! He knows numbers. But instead of showing off his God-given talent to see and sense numbers, he would stop talking and listen. I felt the urge to jump in and say, "Daddy is right," but I had quick flashbacks of light, quick taps on the hands and remembered my place was not in grown folks' conversations. After he patiently listened, he could hear where the misunderstanding lied and could then address just that point so that Mommy could adjust her understanding on her own. It was masterful indeed.

If Daddy hadn't had enough sense to just stop and listen so that he knew what to say, that conversation could have gone on forever and even allowed feelings to be hurt. Instead, he showed me that sometimes it is not about being right, it's about having empathy, being willing to see the other person's perspective, and participating in the dialogue as a helpmate and not a hindrance.

What Daddy was teaching me is a lesson also found in my Heavenly Father's word. The Bible says in Proverbs 25:11-12 that "a word fitly spoken is like apples of gold in settings of silver. Like an earring of gold and an ornament of fine gold is a wise rebuker to an obedient ear" (NKJV). Simply put, know when to shut up. I have to admit, I'm still learning when to yield and often get the urge to be right, but I hear my daddy saying, "Two ears and one mouth." I don't want my words devalued because of inappropriate timing or approach, and when I speak, I want others to feel connected, assured, and God's wisdom through me. It used to bother me to see my daddy not respond or retort, but the entire time, he was modeling discipline, self-control, and patience.

PUT SOME SHOES ON YOUR FEET

As a young child, I always kept a cold or had a sinus infection. It was like clockwork: Martin Luther King Jr. Holiday, the Superbowl, Valentine's Day, and Ashanti's sinus infection. That probably had something to do with the fact that I sucked my thumb from age five to seventeen, and escaping germs was pretty difficult, even when I washed my hands when I got home from school and only sucked my thumb at home. Around the age of thirteen, however, sinus infections took a backseat to getting used to my developing body, and everything didn't feel amazing all the time, especially towards the end of the month. Because daddy was home during the day and afterschool until mommy got home from work, he had the honor of hearing about my ailments and discomforts. I'm not sure why I kept going to him thinking I was going to get any sympathy because he always had the same response. Seriously, every single time, his cure was exactly the same.

If I stubbed my toe, had a fever, broke out in hives, had menstrual cramps or a sore throat, I got the same prescription. Daddy would always look down at my feet, then look at me directly in the eyes and say, "Put some shoes on your feet." Each time, I genuinely expected for the response to be different—for him to offer me a heating pad, an aspirin, a cool cloth for my head, some tea, or a bandage—yet it was always the same song. I'd be confused because he offered his idea with such authority, as if putting shoes on my bare feet would actually stop menstrual cramping. The issue is that I never wore shoes. Even outside.

My family is from the country—North Carolina that is. And even though I was raised in the suburbs of Maryland, I am pretty confident that some of that "down South" energy made it into my DNA. I do not like wearing shoes or being confined by apparel in any way. I actually drive barefoot, which my daddy can't stand. So, I would follow directions and put on some shoes or sometimes just socks, but I never really figured out why he said that until I was an older woman. His answer was enlightening to me. Daddy said, "I told you to put something on your feet because you could catch something more, and not having on shoes could have been the reason sickness was able to enter your body in the first place." Daddy also said he wanted me to put shoes on because something could get stuck in my feet and I could get injured. He would say, "You are no good without your feet." He knew it would resonate with me as a dancer.

While I understood Daddy's perspective a little better, I was admittedly drawn into a few pieces of the explanation. I thought about my Heavenly Father and his armor that He provides for us for the purpose of spiritual warfare. I thought, especially, about Ephesians 6:15 and having the feet shod with the preparation of the Gospel of Peace. You wouldn't go into a battle without shoes, right?

What Daddy Joe was saying made sense all along, and I needed some time to understand it better. When your body is battling an illness, you protect the feet. Have you ever seen someone prepped for surgery without socks? Even women are told to wear warm socks as they are healing from the birthing process. But that's not all. My Heavenly Father just didn't stop at covering my feet, but He also said that my feet should be covered with the preparation of the Gospel of Peace. The Gospel of Peace is the good news found in God's word. When you are prepared with the Gospel of Peace, you know that there is nowhere you will walk that you can't win. Daddy taught me to protect my body from illness, and through that, my Heavenly Father taught me to keep my feet firmly planted in His word.

CLEAN OUT THE VACUUM

Daddies can do everything. Whether it's from their hands or their resources, they can handle it. As a teenager I enjoyed sweeping the carpet in my room, so when I got my own apartment, I carried on the tradition. The problem was that having my own home meant I had way more rooms than one to sweep, but I just kept sweeping. One day, a friend came over and witnessed me feverishly sweeping the carpet in my living room and inquired as to why I didn't have a vacuum. I simply explained that I didn't have one as a child and that sweeping was therapeutic. They convinced me to get one by gifting me one for my birthday. I quickly fell in love with my new toy, which made my life so much easier. I thanked God for giving my friend the wisdom to gift me that mighty vessel—until about three months in.

During one Saturday morning of cleaning, with my gospel music blaring and candles providing a tropical fragrance for the entire house, my new favorite tool did something I had never seen it do before! As I rolled the vacuum over the trash, it would only pick up the larger pieces of trash while leaving the smaller pieces there. But that's not what bothered me. As I pulled the vacuum back over the same spot, the vacuum would just kick the trash out that it just picked up! I instantly got annoyed because my broom never betrayed me this way and I needed to get the floors clean before my girlfriends came over. I suddenly remembered that I was taught to change the bag every so often, and I hadn't done it once yet. I was so proud of myself for changing that bag out and was ready to get the job done. I plugged the vacuum in, rolled it over the exact same spot, and nothing changed. Even more frustrated, I quickly gave up and did what I always do. Since my daddy knows how to do everything, I called him up. He attempted to triage my dilemma over the phone with questions like "Is it plugged in?" and "You aren't trying to pick up paper, are you?" I responded with, "Daddy, I know how to vacuum." My short tone was a clear indication that his presence was requested at my home and not over the phone. Upon arrival, Daddy did his normal survey of the yard and front porch noting that I needed to call the guy to clean my gutters. He can always find something that needs to be addressed that has nothing to do with what I called him over for. Upon his inspection, he affirmed that I did change the vacuum bag correctly, and then he ran the vacuum to experience the exact same debris rejection experience. Then Daddy started to look at parts that I had no clue about. Daddy asked, "When did you last change the filter?" He could tell by my silent voice and loud non-verbal communication from my facial expression that I had no clue as to what he was talking about. Then Daddy took out the filter and showed it to me. It was disgusting and full of gray dirt and build up. It also had a musty odor. Then he started teaching.

"If you don't keep a clean filter, all of the dirt and germs will clog up the vacuum, and it will reject the new debris because it is already full of dirt. Changing the bag does nothing for your problem because with a dirty filter, the trash won't even get to the bag. It's the filter." Daddy did it again. This, too, is a life lesson when it comes to your mindset. It reminded me of how everyone feels the need to come to me with their problems or for help in working out a problem. As a grown woman I understand that it is not healthy to keep accepting others' problems, burdens, and social media posts in my mind because it becomes clutter. Without being intentional about filtering the noise, we block ourselves from being able to take in what we are supposed to receive: love, peace, understanding, patience, and empathy. In fact, we reject it because there is no room for it with the existing filth.

As human beings, we control what we receive, and we have a choice as to what we allow to fester in our minds. Daddy taught me through changing the filter in my vacuum that I also need to filter my life by changing people's access to my peace. At that time, I was extremely short with people, cranky, and more concerned with the impression I felt the need to make with my friends by slaving over this house instead of praying and resting because my friends are just coming to hang out and love on me anyway. Letting go of the "must be seen as" complex is freeing, and being intentional about what I allow in my space is essential. In Philippians 4:8, the Bible says, "Finally, brethren, whatever things are true, whatever things are noble, whatever things are just, whatever things are pure, whatever things are lovely, whatever things are of good report, if there is any virtue and if there is anything praiseworthy—meditate on these things" (NKJV).

Daddy's lessons seem to always parallel our Heavenly Father's word in a way that allows Daddy to teach me from what he knows while God allows me to see the alignment in my life. I thank God for all Girl Dads, but I am really grateful for the one who made me and who is always right there.

When I fell off of my bike trying to fight the cicadas, my daddy was right there.

When I needed supplies for my first time of the month at age twelve, my daddy was right there.

When I had a mouse in my dorm room forty-five miles away, my daddy came to get me and was right there.

When I graduated as the first in our family to finish college, my daddy was right there.

When my car broke down in the middle of the highway, my daddy was right there.

When I had a bumble bee came into my house and I couldn't sleep, my daddy was right there.

When my water broke with my first child and I went into active labor, my daddy was right there.

When I purchased my first car and needed to haggle the price, my daddy was right there.

When I accepted a hand in marriage and said I will always forever, my daddy was right there.

When he broke my heart and left me to figure life out with six kids, my daddy was right there.

When I published my first book and hosted a book launch concert, my daddy was right there.

When I was sick with COVID and didn't think I would make it, my daddy was right there.

When I walked out of the courtroom from divorce proceedings, my daddy was right there.

Today as a divorced daddy's girl, I have returned to his authority and guidance by choice and honor his leadership and covering. I can only imagine the unspoken conversations he has in his head and the strength it takes to share space with a person who broke his baby girl's heart. Yet he does it. That's love. Daddy has taught me to cover my feet while walking in faith, to change the filter while protecting my peace, and to listen more than I speak while presenting an obedient ear. These life lessons have kept me throughout my life in the hardest and lowest times in my life.

THE DADDY'S GIRL CHARGE

As a daddy's girl, I honor my father and cherish the moments we have together. I don't take it for granted that I am blessed to have such an awesome man in my life. As a daddy's girl I will allow each man who comes into my life to be honored for what they uniquely bring, without condemning him for not being just like my daddy. As a daddy's girl, I will be understanding when my mom is in her feelings and not choose sides. As a daddy's girl, I will embody the lessons of love taught by my amazing father while understanding that as much as I want to think my daddy is perfect, he is not. As a daddy's girl, I will not take advantage of my daddy's kindness and strive to engage my independence because Daddy won't always be there.

DEAR SISTER

Dear Sister,

I pray that you realize that no matter what the relationship with your earthly father is that your Heavenly Father has always been there. He will never leave you or forsake you. He made you in His own image and wants nothing more than for you to have an amazing life. Remember that in every season of grief and despair, God allowed it, and if He allowed it, then you can handle it with His support. Know that you have been equipped with everything you need to win the fight, and it is when you surrender to His will that you can find the peace that surpasses all understanding.

EPILOGUE

I've long held that the relationship between a father and a daughter is so important for so many different reasons. Having a daughter myself and loving the fact I was a parent to the degree that I was in the delivery room when my daughter arrived gave me a front-row seat to seeing how important our relationship was going to be.

In witnessing the way the first male in her life—me—related to her mother, my daughter was provided with a template for how she should expect to be treated by a male. The way I spoke to, respected, cared for, and treated her mother was a blueprint for her to follow.

My daughter was also provided with an example of how two people who live together and love each other are supposed to relate to, respect, and coexist with each other. Sadly, a lot of folks don't realize how important the example they set as a couple for their children is. I believe it was Janks Morton who said, "If you're a girl and you have never forgiven your father for whatever serious disconnect you experienced with him, believe it or not, you'll wind up marrying someone just like him." Interestingly enough, Mr. Morton said that sons do

EPILOGUE

the same things with the women who replace their mothers as the "loves of their lives."

It has been theorized that a daughter develops her confidence toward facing the world through the relationship she develops with her father. Somehow, it is easier to summon the necessary courage to take on challenges when you see that your father is firmly in your corner.

Needless to say, I'm extremely proud of the relationship my daughter and I enjoy to this very day.

I'm so pleased to know that I am not alone in these emotions. I encourage you to join me in strengthening the Girl Dad experience through the *Girl Dad: Voices, Lessons, and Reflections of a Black Father on Positive Parenting* Self-Coaching Questions with compassion, reflection, and a desire to appreciate the Girl Dad status.

Dr. Dimitri Conte Kornegay

THE GIRL DAD PLEDGE

As this portion of The Girl Dad Project concludes, you are encouraged to recite the Girl Dad Pledge and engage in further Girl Dad conversations in your village.

AS A GIRL DAD,

- I will remain very knowledgeable about finances, including businesses, home ownership, and investments so that I can teach and model the expectation. (J. Butler)

- I will create lasting memories on which my daughter can reflect later in life and share a laugh, smile, or maybe a warm hug. (G. Clark)

- I will share positive affirmation frames with my daughters as they grow older. (H. McCray)

- I will prioritize time with my family while balancing a growing career. (T. Warner)

- I will fail, learn, grow, and apologize. (J.C. Bryant)

- I will honor my daughter's presence, no matter the circumstances of their conception, and I count it an honor to serve as the protector of my children. (J.O. Bryant)

- I will regularly buy my daughter books that feature positive Black families, girls and women, history, and culture. (J. Davis)

- I will make my coparenting relationship peaceful, healthy, and effective and never speak negatively about my daughter's mom. (K. Burgess)

- I will surround my daughter with love and put her in situations to win. I will be present and involved in every stage of her life. (P. McNair)

- I will make it a priority to spend more time with my daughters while I can. (R. Mack)

- I look forward to the visions and legacies we will create and experience together. (C. Perry)

THE GIRL DAD PLAYBOOK: SELF-COACHING QUESTIONS

As you engage with the powerful stories of fatherhood, use these reflection questions and activities to push your thinking, support you in polishing your parenting, and picture the Girl Dad lifestyle you aim to have for you and your daughter.

PROTECTION

1. What does protection look like for you? What are the similarities and differences in how you show protection to all those you protect? Hint: If you don't know, then ask them. With that information, work to align your understanding so that everyone is getting what they need.

2. In what ways do you seek protection? Do you generally feel protected? How does it make you feel when you don't? Consider the feeling your children may have in moments of not being protected.

3. In the text, Joe gives us an example of how he panicked when he couldn't find his daughter. In what areas of your fatherhood do want to protect more? What is so significant about this area and what can you do to begin strengthening protection?

PRAISE WITH AFFIRMATION

1. Negative self-talk has a greater impact on you than social media or other external criticism. For a day, journal the thoughts that come to your mind about yourself. Evaluate whether they are helpful or harmful.

2. One exercise in combating negative self-talk is to focus on the process as opposed to the product. Rehearse an opportunity to counter negative self-talk of a potential failing task and call out specific parts of the process that are worthy of being affirmed.

3. In what ways can you affirm your daughter beyond beauty? What are some rituals passed down through generations for affirmations? If none, which can you create?

PRAYER OVER EVERYTHING

1. Prayer is a practice of communicating with a higher power of authority in your life. How might you incorporate prayer with your daughter?

2. Many believe in the power of prayer and the law of attraction, which is the belief that positive thoughts yield positive results. What is your experience with either and how do you talk to your daughters about them?

3. What does your practice of prayer and meditation look like? Where did you learn it? How would you like to enhance your quiet time? What are you praying for and believing in your life? Keep a journal of your prayers for forty days, and as prayers are answered, place the date beside them in your journal.

PROMOTE PERSEVERANCE

1. Children hear what we say yet duplicate what they experience with us. "Do what I say and not what I do" is a risky expectation. How have your children witnessed you persevere firsthand?

2. In the text, we read about Greg having to make adjustments to his schedule and advocate for time with his professors just to ensure he could be a husband, father, and full-time student. Do you ask for help when you need to, or do you believe you need to be able to figure the issue out on your own? Give examples and explain the pros and cons of both approaches.

3. Perseverance includes times when we may experience temporary setbacks or failure. What do you to when the task gets hard? What do you need in place in order to get up and keep moving towards the goal?

PURSUE THE PURPOSE

1. From the text, we were reminded of the importance of naming you children. What is the process you used to name your children? How do you support your children to live out the names you've given them?

2. Purpose-driven parenting includes allowing children the opportunity to explore and investigate the world around them. How will you create opportunities from them to pursue their purpose?

PREPARE TO SMILE

1. Life can sometimes present sour scenarios or circumstances, yet we have a choice to find the joy in tough moments. For a week, concentrate on finding the good in every situation (even if it's a lesson learned).

2. It is amazing how many of our mannerisms our children share with us at times beyond strong resemblance. Sometimes we look at them and remember the little us doing the same thing. Take a moment and reflect on those quirky passed-down reminders. Now schedule some time to share them with your child.

3. What made you smile as a child? Create a list of songs, foods, sayings, or special activities that make your child smile. Keep it on hand for future fatherhood moments.

PIVOT INTO POSITION

1. When life brings an unexpected turn of events (even though your actions may have influenced them), what supports do you have in place to help you pivot or bounce back? What resources are available to help you navigate these unexpected happenings?

2. Everyone can benefit from a brotherhood bond that holds you accountable when they veer off course. What does your bond look like? Who is missing? Who needs to go?

3. Oftentimes, a pivot means going in another direction without looking back. In what areas should you keep moving forward without looking back? How will you be intentional about letting go of distractions that can prevent your progress?

PRESSURE COOKER

1. Men, specifically men of color, have extreme amounts of pressure to perform placed on them. What are some of those pressures and how, as men, can we address and assess them in a healthy way?

2. The Bible says in Matthew 25:21, "His master said to him, 'Well done, good and faithful servant. ... You have been faithful over a little; I will set you over much.

Enter into the joy of your master" (ESV). In what areas of life do you need to display faithfulness over what you already have?

3. The Hedonic treadmill is the tendency of pursing pleasure after pleasure without satisfaction. As you pursue, reflect on areas of contentment in your life. Where can you identify areas of happiness and joy with where you are in life?

4. Sometimes the pressures of life start with us and the need to be seen a certain way.

   a) Make a list of everything you are responsible for.

   b) Return to the list and circle every task/responsibility that is non-negotiable.

   c) Return to the marked list and put names beside responsibilities that others can take on.

   d) Return to the marked list and highlight responsibilities that you take on that are not essential and that keep you from doing the non-negotiables in excellence.

   e) For the items with names, meet with the best qualified and train them to assume that responsibility.

f) For the items highlighted, make a plan of action indicating how you will remove yourself from the responsibility (which may include training someone else and giving appropriate notice that you will no longer serve in that capacity).

g) Use the reclaimed time to reinvest in your family dynamics.

POWER IN THE PAUSE

1. Rest and rejuvenation activities can be the perfect relaxed environment needed for families to focus on one another. How do you (or do you want to) pause and connect with your family?

2. Although the past is the past and you cannot change it, there is strength in pausing to reflect on past behaviors and how they are connected to current behaviors. On your own, write a letter to a brand-new Girl Dad with what you learned about being a Girl Dad through your past experiences.

3. In the text, we are encouraged to say three power phrases: "I'm sorry," "I'm blew it," and "Please forgive me." Behind that request for forgiveness is not just acknowledgement but changed behavior moving forward. What keeps you from apologizing sometimes? How can you overcome the circumstance and apologize?

PRESENCE OVER PRESENTS

1. Think back to your childhood and reflect on when someone's presence meant so much more to you than the presents or tangible items that may have come along with it. What about their presence brought you joy?

2. Understanding that you are one person and may not be physically present at every single "first time" in your children's lives, what steps can be taken to ensure them of your love from a distance? How can a non-custodial or long-distance Girl Dad still have an impact on their children's lives from afar?

3. Make a list of ten to twelve activities or lessons you want to teach each of your daughters in the next year. Place each one in an envelope. Monthly or whenever you feel the urge to by a present to overcompensate for your absence, remember these envelopes and allow your daughter to select one to choose presence over presents.

PRODIGAL GIRL DADS PROSPER

1. It is inevitable that we will miss the mark at times in our parenting. One way we teach is through modeling behaviors that we want our children to emulate. As you survey your fatherhood journey, identify areas in your life where your lifestyle contradicts your di-

rections. What are they? Where is there room to align your behavior and your child rearing?

2. Personal pleasures can impact our role as a father when we give too much weight to the pleasure. As you navigate in this journey, what personal pleasures may be impeding your progress as a Girl Dad? How might you prioritize your pleasures and, as a principle, honor responsibility over the pleasure?

3. Prodigal can be defined as one who returned after an absence. Even the father that is visibly seen daily can be absent. At the same time, a father who can't be seen in person daily can be present. How do you remain visible in your daughter's life? Where can your daughter feel your presence throughout the day?

PAY ATTENTION

1. Sometimes life lessons are nestled within the normal routines of daily life. With life being so fast paced, ignoring these opportunities to apply practical principles is not a surprise. When you think about it, fishing teaches patience, for example. In what other normal routines or activities can you find life lessons? Make a plan to be intentional about sharing them with your family.

2. In the text, the author realizes that when communicating with potential suitors, daddy's girls actually look

for and are attracted to the qualities of their father. What qualities would your daughter be looking for in her mate today?

3. The author remarks that although her daddy was there to do anything she needed him to, he also taught her to do things for herself and be independent. Have your daughter make a list of thirty things she wants to learn to do, and you make your list of thirty skills you want to teach her. Compare notes and enjoy the daddy-daughter time learning these skills.

ABOUT THE AUTHORS

JOSEPH O. BRYANT

Joseph O. Bryant is a native of North Carolina and the youngest of three sons. Growing up, Joseph enjoyed playing percussion and being outdoors. He continued to march to beat of his own drum after graduation, when he moved to the "big city" and married his high school sweetheart, Helen.

Joseph claimed his Girl Dad status in 1978, when his daughter Ashanti was born. Joe raised his family in the home they built after welcoming his only son, Joseph. During this time, Joe played softball with community leagues and was known for his smooth, hand-dancing moves. In 1994, he got his Girl Dad promotion at age forty-five when his baby girl, Mariyah, was born.

After forty-seven years of service to the United States Postal Service, Joe spends his retirement enjoying his nine grandchildren, sports, his garden, and his bride of fifty years.

To connect, email him at joscarbryant@gmail.com

DR. HAROLD A. MCCRAY, JR.

Dr. Harold A. McCray, Jr. was born and raised in Philadelphia, PA. Upon his graduation from Delaware State University with a bachelor's in political science, Dr. McCray started his career as a sixth-grade classroom teacher with Prince George's County Public Schools. During his fourteen-year career with Prince George's County Public Schools, he also served as instructional lead teacher (ILT), district math resource teacher, assistant principal, resident principal, and principal. He also received his master's degree from Bowie State University and a doctorate from Walden University.

Dr. McCray has written curricula, mentored aspiring administrators, and presented at various national education conferences. Dr. McCray has a strong belief that a learning environment should be one in which students feel safe and supported, which is conducive to receiving a high-quality education. He currently serves as the principal of Stanton Elementary School in Washington, DC.

Learn more at www.drhspeaks.org

DEACON JEFFREY BUTLER

Jeffrey Butler was born and raised in the Washington, DC, metropolitan area. His family and faith are the priorities in his life. Jeffrey is married to Pamela McCollum-Butler and is a father of three adult children: Pamela, Crystal, and Jeffrey. He is a member of First Baptist Church of Glenarden International, where he is a deacon and scoutmaster of Boy Scout Troop 1657. He is also a mentor in the men's ministry as well as the couples' ministry. When he is not spending time with the Boy Scouts and ministry, he enjoys quietly relaxing at home with his wife of thirty-two years. Jeffrey enjoys being outdoors—camping, hiking, or biking—as a way to ground and reconnect with Christ. He is an alumnus of University of Maryland and Bowie State universities. He is also a member of the Alpha Phi Alpha Fraternity Incorporated.

To connect, email him at butler.971423@gmail.com

GREGORY CLARK

Gregory Clark is a professional in the finance industry and a co-owner of Clark Premier Realty Group, LLC along with his wife, Cherice, servicing clients in the District of Columbia, Maryland and Virginia. Active in his community, he is a youth football coach/mentor and enjoys helping guide youth in the realm of sports through local organizations in Prince George's County, Maryland. He holds a Master of Business Administration and is a proud alumnus of Howard University, where he graduated with a degree in finance. Raised as a "military brat," he grew up in a small town in Southeast Georgia and has resided in the DC metropolitan area for close to thirty years. Above all, he relishes in being a positive and proud man of faith, a loving and supporting husband, the ultimate Girl Dad to his amazing daughters, and a devoted "PaPa" to his adorable grandchildren.

Learn more at www.gregoryjclark.com

ABOUT THE AUTHORS

JULIUS DAVIS

Julius Davis, Ed.D., is the University System of Maryland (USM) Wilson H. Elkins Associate Professor of Mathematics Education and founding director of the Center for Research and Mentoring of Black Male Students and Teachers at Bowie State University. He is a Black father scholar who believes in raising Black girls with a strong racial, ethnic, cultural, gender, and educational identity rooted in Black history and culture. He is a devoted husband and father of four children—three boys and one girl.

To connect, email him at jldavis@bowiestate.edu

JOSEPH C. BRYANT

Joseph Bryant is a native of Prince George's County, Maryland and now lives in Howard County, Maryland with his wife, Tenisha, and their three children, Norah, Johannah, and Quentin. With a bachelor of science in business management from Morgan State University, Joseph has been working for the federal government since 2006. Joseph is a brother of the Eta Gamma Chapter of Kappa Kappa Psi National Honorary Band Fraternity. He is also a trained voice actor. Joseph approaches his writing with honesty and humor.

Learn more at www.joebryantwrites.com

PHILLIP MCNAIR

Philip McNair is currently leading the Future of Work Initiative at the National Institutes of Health (NIH). His role as project manager is to oversee the changing dynamics of how work, workers, and the workplace will evolve as a result of the COVID-19 pandemic. Early in Philip's career, he served in the United States Navy, where he decommissioned the USS Hawes (FFG-53) and pre-commissioned the USS Gravely (DDG-107). Since his departure from active duty in 2012, Philip has held positions at Amazon Web Services (AWS) and Conquest Solutions, an engineering consulting firm based out of Maryland. He holds an MS in systems engineering from the George Washington University and a PMP® certification. Other notable ventures include the current development of his app, Parkly, and his hat company, NoMan Hat Co., based out of Washington, DC. During Philip's down time, he enjoys exercising and spending time with family and friends.

To connect, email him at PhilipDMcNair@gmail.com

REGINALD MACK

Reginald Otis Mack was born on August 4, 1978, in Washington, DC, to Robert and Cecilia Mack. He was raised in Prince George's County, Maryland. While attending Kettering Middle School, he was introduced to his passion of acting in drama class. He would later audition for a local television series titled *Right Turns Only!* He won the role as a supporting cast member. After middle school, he attended Largo High School, and during his senior year, he was voted homecoming king.

After high school, Reginald went to Prince George's Community College and studied business, writing, and psychology. He eventually found his way into the culinary field and developed a deeper love for food and serving others. With his charm and entrepreneurial spirit, he began to cook for local celebrities and athletes. He has four wonderful kids for whom he works hard to make sure they are on the right path.

Learn more at www.ChefROM.tv

KELLY BURGESS

Kelly Scott Burgess is a 2019 PGCPS Teacher of the Year finalist, currently working as the AVID coordinator and elective teacher at Dwight D. Eisenhower MS in Prince George's County, Maryland. He also teaches music privately, specializing in violin, viola, and cello.

A native Washingtonian, Kelly received his bachelor of arts in music education from the University of Maryland. He is currently pursuing a graduate degree in curriculum and instruction with an emphasis in TESOL Education. The twenty-five-year veteran of public education says, "Teaching is like tending plants in a garden. Place them both in good soil with regular water, light, and nutrients, and they will grow."

In his spare time, he enjoys reading; gardening; music; exercising; and spending time with his wife, children, and grandchildren. He resides in Mount Rainier, Maryland, with his wife, Pamela, and their dog and cat.

To connect, email him at kscottburgess@yahoo.com

THOMAS G. WARNER, JR.

Thomas G. Warner, Jr. is a native of Atlanta, Georgia and a product of Atlanta Public Schools. He is a graduate of Morris Brown College in Atlanta where he earned a bachelor of arts in music and music education. Thomas also attended Florida State University College of Music (master of music education) and is currently a candidate for the doctor of philosophy in music education from the University of North Carolina at Greensboro. He is a nationally sought-after author and clinician.

He is the Assistant Director of University Bands and a music lecturer at North Carolina Agricultural and Technical State University. He holds several professional music organization memberships, some of which include executive leadership roles, and is a member of Alpha Phi Alpha Fraternity Inc., Kappa Kappa Psi Band Fraternity, Phi Mu Alpha Sinfonia, Prince Hall Masonry United Supreme Council 32°, and The Ancient Egyptian Arabic Order Nobles of the Mystic Shrine.

Learn more at www.OneFiveOneProductions.com

ABOUT THE AUTHORS

DR. CHARLES LUCIOUS PERRY

Dr. Charles Lucious Perry was born in Lake City, Florida, on July 9, 1954. He is a twenty-year United States Air Force personnel and human resource technician, supervisor, and analyst retiree. He holds a bachelor's degree in political science from Mercer University, a master's degree in public administration from Georgia College, and a doctor of management from the University of Maryland Global Campus. From 1992 to 2018, Charles worked as an academician, consultant, resource developer, training director, and entrepreneur. He has provided support in helping to start, lead, manage, sustain and evaluate organizations. Charles's strengths are in project management, organizational development, strategic planning, program evaluation, and board retreat facilitation. Charles is an active and dedicated member of Metropolitan Baptist Church and has served faithfully on a number of the church's boards, choirs, and committees. Charles has four college-graduate adult children and five grandchildren.

To connect, email him at CPerryumuc@aol.com

ASHANTI BRYANT FOSTER

Dr. Ashanti Bryant Foster is an accomplished educator of over 20 years and mother of six residing in Prince George's County, Maryland. She is a graduate of Morgan State University, Bowie State University, and Argosy University. Ashanti was a 2010 Teacher of the Year finalist and served as the 2016 Maryland Assistant Principal of the Year during her public school tenure. She now leads the teacher education department at a local college where she recruits and prepares future educators.

Ashanti is also a strengths-based coach and trainer, facilitating sessions for teachers on student engagement. She coaches youth and women in leadership and life skills through scouting, community programs, and positive psychology. Her first book, *Armed to Surrender*, aims to foster the belief in readers that life doesn't have to be perfect to be amazing as she shares testimonies of triumphant trials and redefines bravery and strength.

Learn more at DrAshantiSays.com

CREATING DISTINCTIVE BOOKS WITH INTENTIONAL RESULTS

We're a collaborative group of creative masterminds with a mission to produce high-quality books to position you for monumental success in the marketplace.

Our professional team of writers, editors, designers, and marketing strategists work closely together to ensure that every detail of your book is a clear representation of the message in your writing.

Want to know more?
Write to us at info@publishyourgift.com
or call (888) 949-6228

Discover great books, exclusive offers, and more at
www.PublishYourGift.com

Connect with us on social media

@publishyourgift

www.ingramcontent.com/pod-product-compliance
Lightning Source LLC
Chambersburg PA
CBHW072005070526
44583CB00015B/1349